CLASSIC

STAR WARS

ESCAPE TO HOTH

introduction
Al Williamson

art assist
Allen Nunis

colorists
Steve Buccellato
Matthew Hollingsworth
Ray Murtaugh
Tom Roberts

---

series editors
Bob Cooper
Anina Bennett

collection editor
Lynn Adair

collection designer
Scott Tice

collection design manager
Brian Gogolin

MIKE RICHARDSON
publisher

NEIL HANKERSON
executive vp

MARK COX
art director

DAVID SCROGGY
vp of publishing

SEAN TIERNEY
computer graphics director

LOU BANK
vp of sales & marketing

CHRIS CREVISTON
director of accounting

ANDY KARABATSOS
vp of finance

MICHAEL MARTENS
marketing director

MARK ANDERSON
general counsel

TOD BORLESKE
sales & licensing director

RANDY STRADLEY
creative director

MARK ELLINGTON
director of operations

CINDY MARKS
director of production & design

DALE LAFOUNTAIN
director of m.i.s.

special thanks to
Lucy Autrey Wilson
& Allan Kausch
at Lucasfilm Licensing

CLASSIC
STAR WARS®
ESCAPE TO HOTH

by
Archie Goodwin
and
Al Williamson

DARK HORSE COMICS®

STAR WARS TRADE PAPERBACKS AVAILABLE FROM DARK HORSE

CLASSIC STAR WARS
Volume One
Volume Two: The Rebel Storm
Volume Three: Escape to Hoth
A New Hope
The Empire Strikes Back
Return of the Jedi

DARK EMPIRE I & II

DROIDS
The Kalarba Adventures

TALES OF THE JEDI

CLASSIC STAR WARS® VOLUME THREE

This book is based on the classic Star Wars® newspaper strip and collects
issues 15-20 of the Dark Horse comic-book series *Classic Star Wars*.

Published by
Dark Horse Comics, Inc.
10956 SE Main Street
Milwaukie, OR 97222

January 1996
First edition
ISBN:1-56971-093-7

2 4 6 8 10 9 7 5 3 1

Printed in Canada

A Tale of Flash and Luke

(or My Connection to *Star Wars*)

by Al Williamson

The artwork assembled in this volume collects the strips from the end of Archie Goodwin's and my three-year-and-one-month run of producing the daily and Sunday *Star Wars* newspaper strip. Archie and I had started doing the strip in 1981. We were very pleased with the material as we produced it, and we hoped that the people at Lucasfilm would be, too.

It is hard to believe more than ten years have passed since we ended our work on *Star Wars*. The story behind my involvement with *Star Wars* is an intertwining tale spanning many years of myself, *Flash Gordon*, and Alex Raymond. As a child growing up in Bogota, Colombia, I saw *Flash Gordon Conquers the Universe* starring Buster Crabbe. There, in the darkened theater, up on the screen were adventure and excitement like I had never seen or experienced before. I fell in love with Flash Gordon through Buster Crabbe. Flash Gordon was real to me. He was my hero, in the form of Buster Crabbe.

Sketch by Al Williamson

This serial led me to discover Alex Raymond who created Flash Gordon in 1934 for King Features syndicate. Raymond was arguably the greatest "figure man" who ever drew comics. He truly believed in the world he created, and it showed in every panel of every strip he ever drew. When Raymond's "Flash Gordon" pages appeared each Sunday, millions of viewers got to see Flash encounter all sorts of adventures. Flash was the ultimate hero, always battling the forces of evil. He was straightforward and true in his nobility of purpose. There were no "grey areas" to Flash Gordon.

The movies also provided me with great escapism and enjoyment. My friends and I spent countless hours viewing such films as *Gunga Din*, *King Kong*, *Scaramouche*, and *King Solomon's Mines*. Any Errol Flynn film we always went to see, but particularly *The Adventures of Robin Hood*, *The Sea Hawk*, *Objective Burma*, *Dodge City*, and *The Adventures of Don Juan*. Flynn, along with Stewart Granger, was absolutely the best at the swashbuckling/adventure-type thing. And many of the "B" westerns also filled the bill. These movies fired my imagination, filling my need for excitement and drama.

As I developed as an artist, I tried to imitate Alex Raymond's work. I suppose I should say *emulate* instead of *imitate*, because I always added something of my own to the work. Raymond's work continues to inspire me to this day.

A couple of years after my comics career began, I started working for EC Comics, most of my work being for the science-fiction titles *Weird Science* and *Weird Fantasy*. I had fun drawing these stories and tried to bring them that mystical quality of excitement and drama that I had seen in *Flash Gordon* and the other films.

Totally unknown to me at the time, a boy named George Lucas was reading and enjoying my comics work.

In New York in 1956, I first met Archie while he was in art school. We became friends. Archie wrote several stories that I drew for Harvey Comics and later got me involved with the Warren titles *Eerie* and *Creepy* for which he wrote and edited.

In the mid-1960s, I did some *Flash Gordon* comics for King Features, and again Archie wrote some of the scripts. This later led to our teaming up to produce the daily strip "Secret Agent X-9" for King Features. Starting in January 1967, we worked together on this strip until February 1980. To me, Archie is the best — I mean the very best — writer in comics! I have never had trouble with any of his scripts. He is my favorite writer, and he's spoiled me for working with anyone else.

I was approached in the mid-1970s by a man named Ed Summer. He had a friend who was making a science-fiction movie. This friend liked my work and wanted to know if I would be interested in doing a comic-book adaptation of the film. I had never heard of the movie or the director but that didn't matter. I was still doing the daily "X-9" strip as well as the Sunday "Big Ben Bolt" strip, and any additional work was just impossible.

The director, of course, turned out to be George Lucas and the film was, of course, Star Wars.

When I saw *Star Wars*, I was spellbound by the beauty of the thing. George went on to create a wonderful trilogy of stories that were exciting, fun, and family oriented — totally refreshing for the time. In retrospect, it was nice to see something done with heroes who were noble and inspiring instead of with the dark-centered characters and so-called heroes we are so flooded with today. Even Darth Vader in the end tried to make up for his wrongdoing.

After viewing Star Wars, I couldn't believe or understand why the guy who made this liked my work. It left me quite puzzled.

I was again approached in 1977 about doing a "Star Wars" daily strip, but because of my contract commitments with King Features, I again had to turn down the opportunity.

Archie and I parted company from "X-9" and King Features in 1980 after a monetary dispute. We had been offered the comics adaptation for *The Empire Strikes Back* with Marvel Comics, and here began my association with the *Star Wars* saga. When I got my photo stills from Lucasfilm to begin working on the

adaptation, I could instantly see George Lucas' attraction to Alex Raymond's work and thus our mutual admiration for Raymond and *Flash Gordon*. Flash and Luke Skywalker were twin brothers of different molds! Both held an unerring purpose to battle injustice. Lucasfilm was pleased with Archie's and my adaptation and again they offered us the daily strip. I'd committed myself to doing the comic-book adaptation of the *Flash Gordon* movie, but after that, I finally got to start work on the "Star Wars" strip. As they say, "The third time's the charm."

I didn't know it until years later, but some time before *Star Wars* was made, George Lucas approached King Features with an offer to make a feature film of *Flash Gordon*. As we now know, this never happened. But since he couldn't make *Flash Gordon*, drawing some inspiration from Raymond's work, George instead made *Star Wars*.

If George had made a *Flash Gordon* film, oh, what a film it would have been! Filled with excitement and drama — good versus evil — why, it would have been . . . *Star Wars*!

I have always been extremely grateful to George for the chance to do this strip and to be associated with something as wonderful as *Star Wars*. I worked extremely hard to create the best art of which I was capable. I still feel it is some of my finest.

I am also always grateful to work with Archie Goodwin. Archie writes highly intelligent scripts, creating stories that I believe people want to read. His dialogue is outstanding; his people talk the way people *really do* talk. Archie does a first-rate job and weaves a story that leaves you wanting more.

I hope you enjoy reading these stories as much as I enjoyed drawing them. It was very rewarding working on *Star Wars*, and I hope the work still holds up under the passage of time.

—Al Williamson
September 1995

WHAT HAS COME BEFORE

As our Rebel heroes attempt to surprise the Imperial troops on fogbound Daluuj, Han rigs a skimmer to blow up in their midst. Meanwhile, the Mon Calamari Admiral Ackbar devises a plan to draw the Imperials across the center of the lake where the Millennium Falcon lies submerged, so that the giant sea worms attack their skimmers — at the same time setting the Falcon free. As the Rebels escape Daluuj, a battle is joined between the Executor and a Rebel battle cruiser. After quickly dispatching the Rebel ship, Darth Vader continues toward the Rebels' Yavin base, leaving a series of Rebel ships strewn in his wake. Upon reaching Yavin Base, General Dodonna confides that he believes his son, Vrad, was lost in a failed attempt to stop Vader. This same scout ship, which Luke thinks he spotted sneaking away from the battle with Vader, subsequently crash lands on Yavin Four. Reunited with his son, General Dodonna asks for volunteers for a "doom mission" to stop Vader. Both Vrad and Luke volunteer, and before Luke can voice his doubts about Vrad's loyalty, the two promptly get in a tussle, with Vrad admitting that Luke's suspicions about his loyalties were right.

MAYBE I FLED THE *ENEMY* LAST MISSION, SKYWALKER...BUT I CAN STILL TEACH YOU SOMETHING ABOUT *FIGHTING!*

FIRST LESSON IS GOING TO BE *PAINFUL*: NEVER LET YOUR *FOE* GET THE ADVANTAGE!

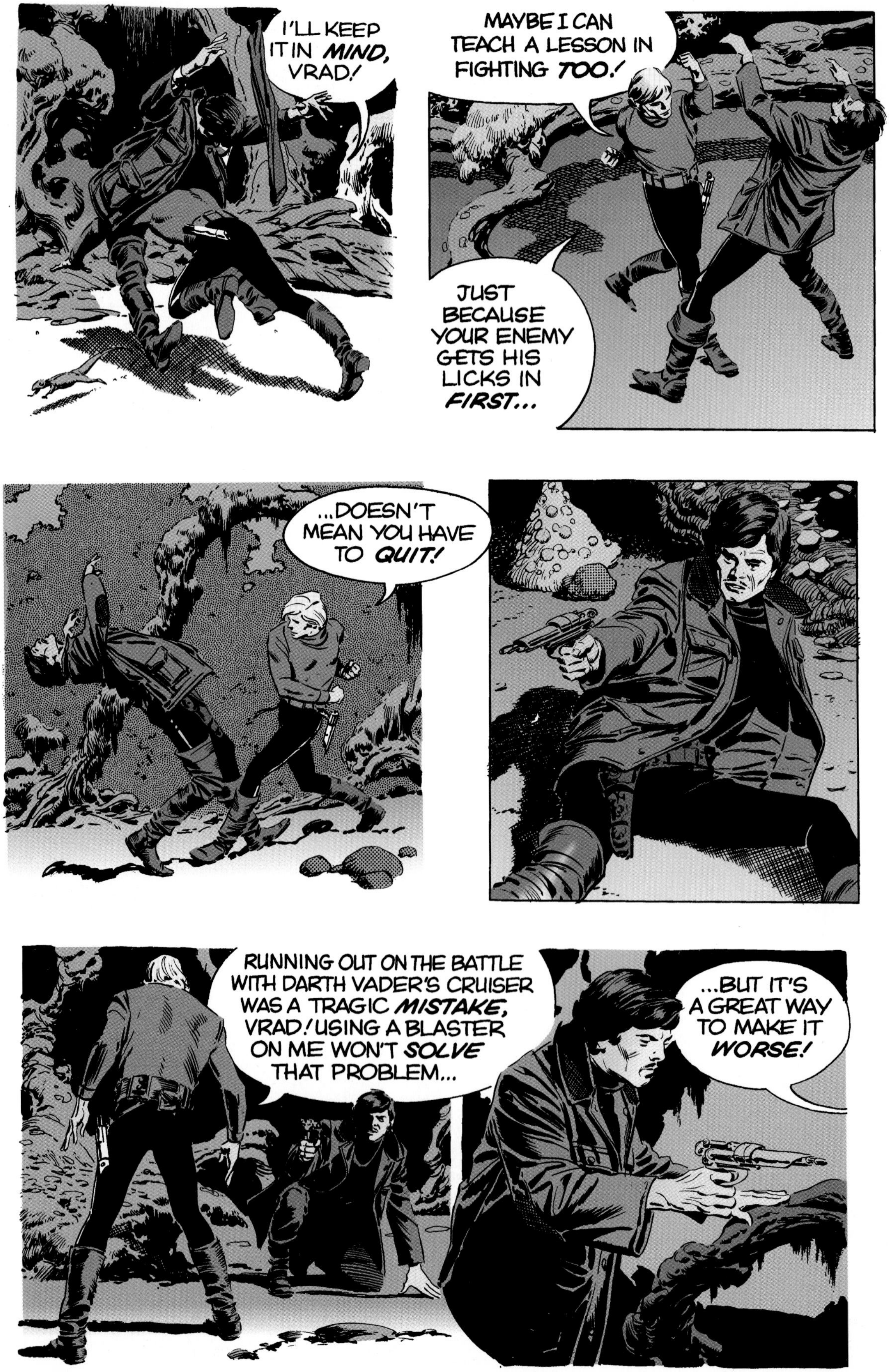
I'LL KEEP IT IN MIND, VRAD!
MAYBE I CAN TEACH A LESSON IN FIGHTING TOO!
JUST BECAUSE YOUR ENEMY GETS HIS LICKS IN FIRST...
...DOESN'T MEAN YOU HAVE TO QUIT!
RUNNING OUT ON THE BATTLE WITH DARTH VADER'S CRUISER WAS A TRAGIC MISTAKE, VRAD! USING A BLASTER ON ME WON'T SOLVE THAT PROBLEM...
...BUT IT'S A GREAT WAY TO MAKE IT WORSE!

OKAY, SKYWALKER...YOU WIN *THIS* ROUND! BUT I'M NOT TURNING MYSELF IN FOR *FLEEING* THAT BATTLE...

...AND I'M NOT *QUITTING* OUR MISSION AGAINST DARTH VADER!

Vrad Dodonna stalks away toward the Yavin base landing field...

YOU AND CHEWIE CAN COME *OUT* NOW, HAN! THANKS FOR TRAILING AFTER ME...

...EVEN IF I *DIDN'T* NEED THE HELP!

TAKES *SHARP SENSES* TO SPOT US, KID...WHY DON'T THEY WARN YOU *AWAY* FROM THIS MISSION WITH DODONNA?!

MAYBE YOU CAN'T *PROVE* IT, BUT THE GENERAL'S SON'S GONE *BAD!* ANY MISSION WITH HIM IS A *DOOM MISSION!*

BUT THE *REBEL ALLIANCE* IS DOOMED IF IT *FAILS,* HAN!

And shortly, when the attack ship that will strike at Darth Vader's giant cruiser takes off...

...Luke Skywalker is in it *WITH* Vrad Dodonna!

THERE IT *GOES*, ARTOO...OUR FORCES' *LAST HOPE* FOR STOPPING THAT MONSTROUS *SHIP* OF DARTH VADER'S!

VEE-DOOTA BRR-WHEET!

WHY WEREN'T *YOU* THE DESIGNATED ASTRO-DROID ABOARD*?* AS FIRST PILOT, *VRAD DODONNA* MADE THE DECISION, *NOT* MASTER LUKE...

SURELY, YOU DON'T QUESTION THE JUDGMENT OF A *GENERAL'S* SON*?!*

On a monitor screen in Rebel headquarters... a ship soars spaceward!

NOT MUCH TO SEND AGAINST DARTH VADER'S NEW *STAR DESTROYER*, GENERAL DODONNA!

IT HAS THE *POWER GEM,* PRINCESS...

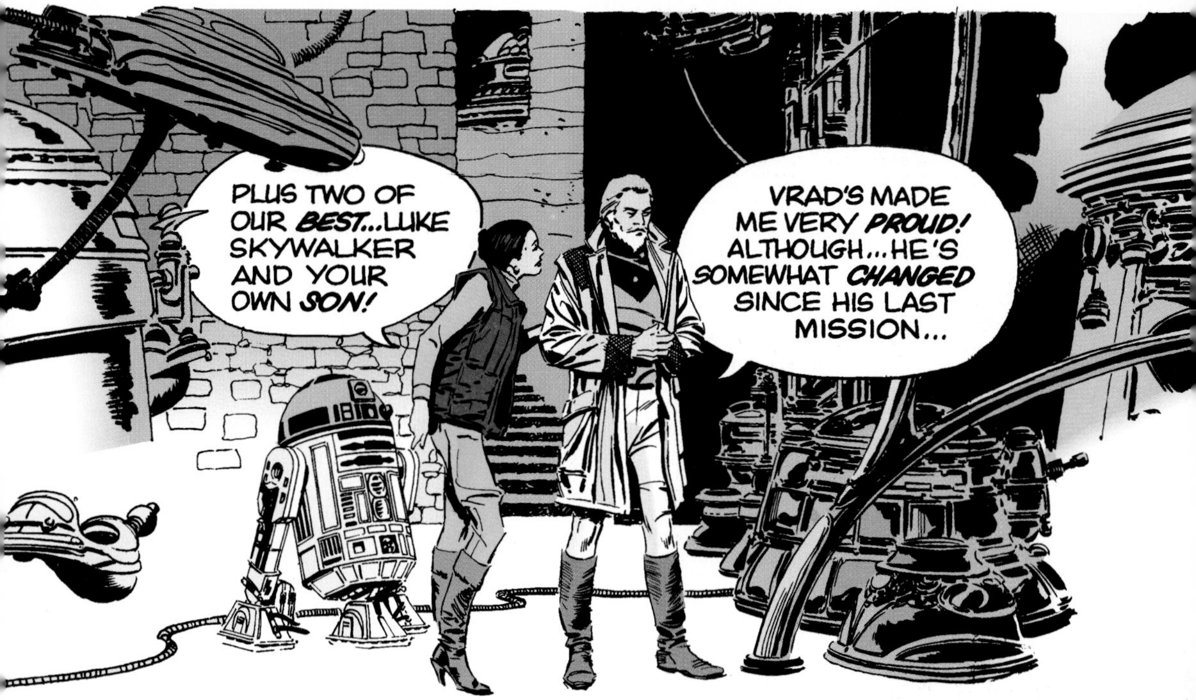
PLUS TWO OF OUR BEST...LUKE SKYWALKER AND YOUR OWN SON!
VRAD'S MADE ME VERY PROUD! ALTHOUGH...HE'S SOMEWHAT CHANGED SINCE HIS LAST MISSION...

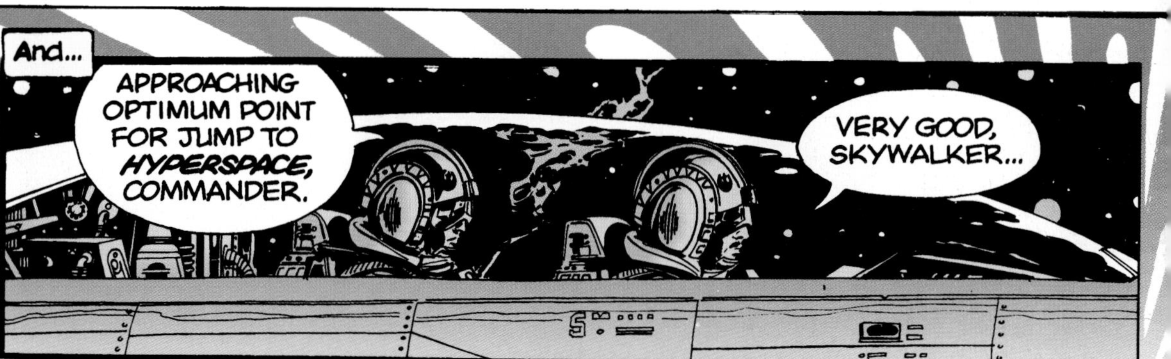
And...
APPROACHING OPTIMUM POINT FOR JUMP TO HYPERSPACE, COMMANDER.
VERY GOOD, SKYWALKER...

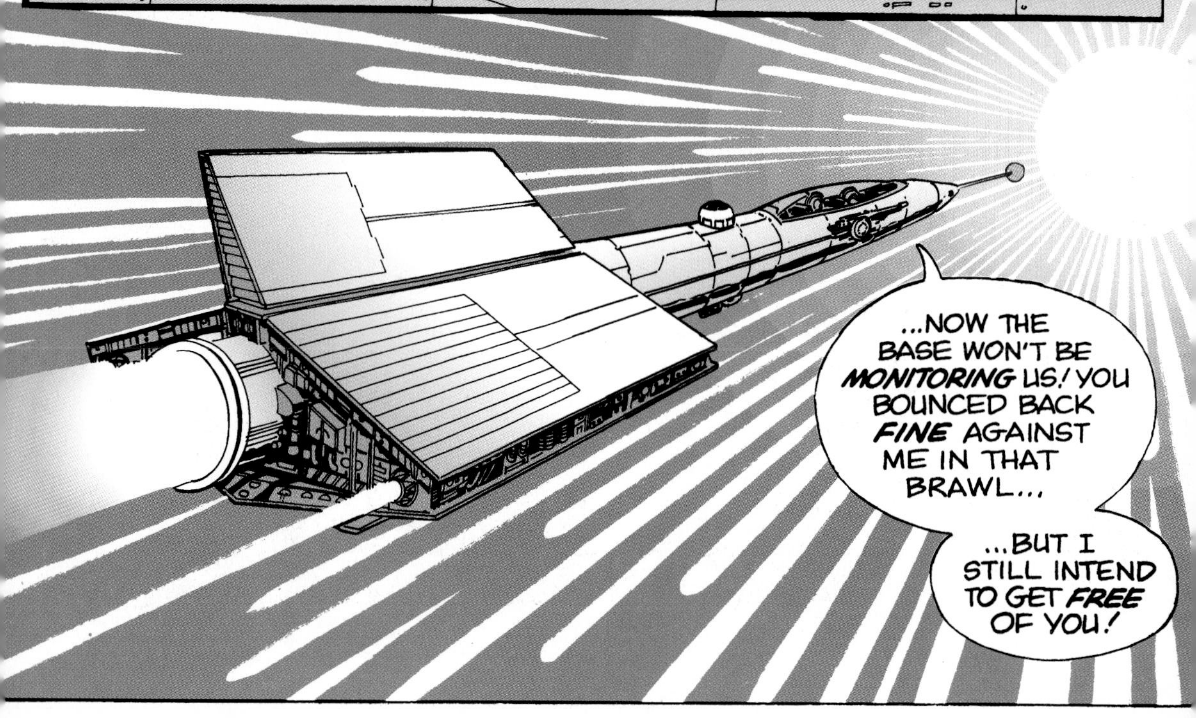
...NOW THE BASE WON'T BE MONITORING US! YOU BOUNCED BACK FINE AGAINST ME IN THAT BRAWL...
...BUT I STILL INTEND TO GET FREE OF YOU!

I NEVER *WANTED* YOU ON THIS MISSION SKYWALKER... I *STILL* DON'T!

I'M HERE TO *HELP*, VRAD! YOU MADE A *MISTAKE* IN YOUR FIRST TRY AT DARTH VADER'S CRUISER...THIS IS A CHANCE TO SET IT *STRAIGHT!*

IT'S A *CHANCE* ALL RIGHT, HERO...AND I MEAN TO MAKE THE MOST OF IT!

The Rebel vessel drops from hyperspace...

NO HEAT PARTICLE INDICATIONS, VRAD...DARTH VADER'S SHIP HASN'T CROSSED THIS SECTOR YET!

WITH ALL THESE PLANETOIDS FOR *COVER*, IT'S A *PERFECT SPOT* FOR OUR ATTACK!

EXCITED, SKYWALKER? YOU SHOULD BE *AFRAID.*

IN A FEW SECONDS, WE'LL BE FACING A *MONSTER!* IT BROKE *ME*--GENERAL DODONNA'S SON.

IT COULD HAPPEN TO *YOU*, HERO!

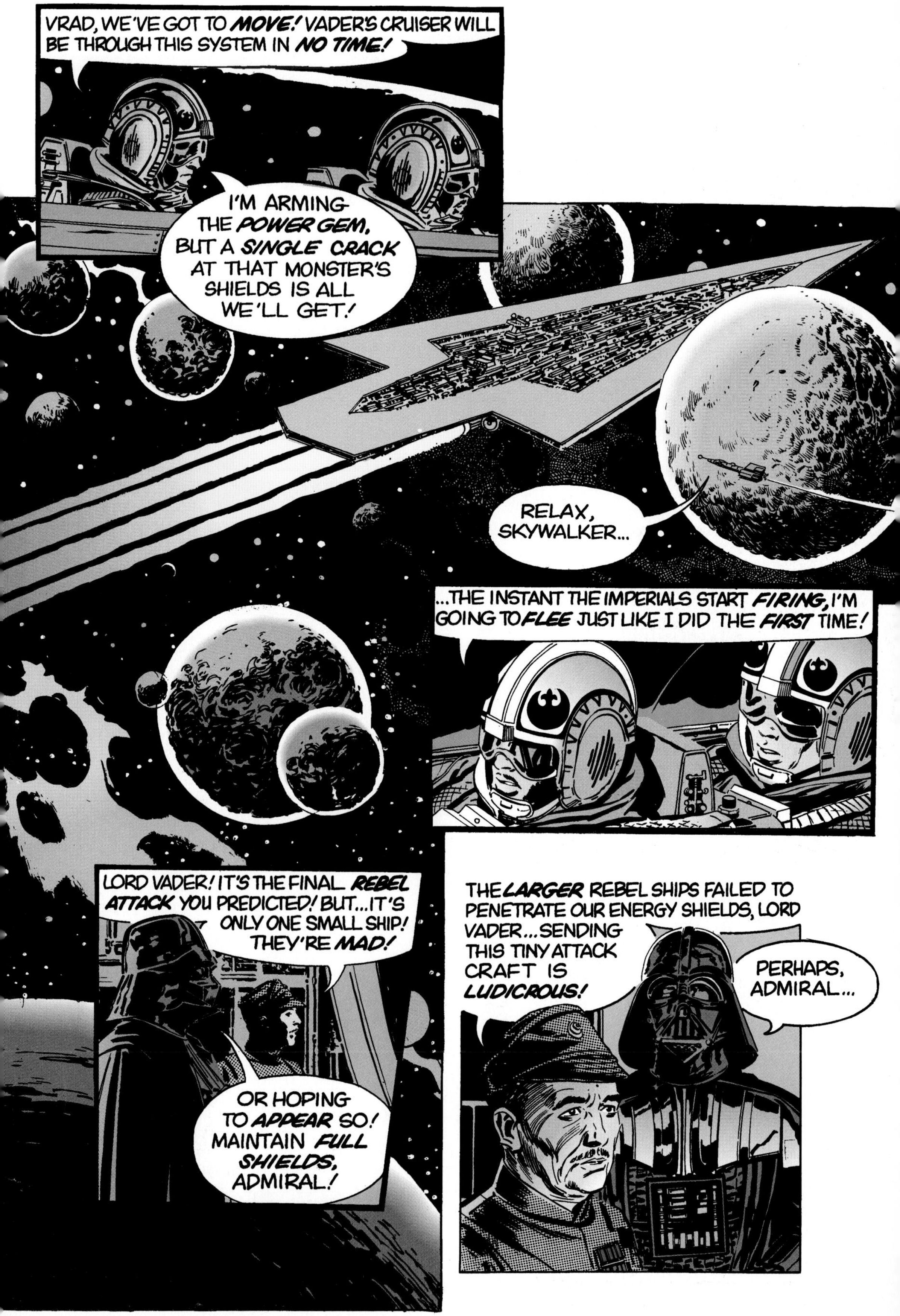
VRAD, WE'VE GOT TO MOVE! VADER'S CRUISER WILL BE THROUGH THIS SYSTEM IN NO TIME!
I'M ARMING THE POWER GEM, BUT A SINGLE CRACK AT THAT MONSTER'S SHIELDS IS ALL WE'LL GET!
RELAX, SKYWALKER...
...THE INSTANT THE IMPERIALS START FIRING, I'M GOING TO FLEE JUST LIKE I DID THE FIRST TIME!
LORD VADER! IT'S THE FINAL REBEL ATTACK YOU PREDICTED! BUT...IT'S ONLY ONE SMALL SHIP! THEY'RE MAD!
OR HOPING TO APPEAR SO! MAINTAIN FULL SHIELDS, ADMIRAL!
THE LARGER REBEL SHIPS FAILED TO PENETRATE OUR ENERGY SHIELDS, LORD VADER...SENDING THIS TINY ATTACK CRAFT IS LUDICROUS!
PERHAPS, ADMIRAL...

...BUT IN CASE IT'S *NOT*, ORDER OUR GUNNERS TO *OPEN FIRE!*

ATTACK! Luke and Vrad Dodonna's special craft zooms toward Darth Vader's huge new battle cruiser! But...

YOU *CAN'T* TURN AWAY, VRAD... NOT *NOW!* I'VE ARMED THE *POWER GEM*... ITS AURA IS *DRAINING!*

IF WE DON'T USE IT *SOON*, IT'LL BE TOO WEAK TO *EVER* PENETRATE THAT MONSTER'S SHIELDS!

WE CAME CLOSE ENOUGH FOR THEM TO *FEEL* IT, SKYWALKER! THAT'S *ALL* I WANT... EXCEPT FOR GETTING RID OF *YOU!*

Maneuvered wildly by Vrad Dodonna, the special Rebel attack ship successfully *FLEES* the monstrous cruiser, *EXECUTOR!*

LORD VADER! INSTRUMENTS INDICATE THAT TINY CRAFT NEARLY *PENETRATED* OUR SHIELD! WHAT COULD IT *HAVE* THAT--

A *POWER GEM!* AND SOMETHING *MORE* INTERESTING...

ALL *POWER GEMS* WERE DESTROYED DURING THE DAYS OF THE OLD REPUBLIC, LORD VADER!

EVIDENTLY, THE REBELS FOUND AT LEAST *ONE* THAT WASN'T FOR THEIR ATTACK SHIP...

...BUT I AM *MORE* INTERESTED IN THE FACT THAT SOMEONE *ABOARD* THE CRAFT IS TOUCHED BY THE *FORCE!*

Abandoning the attack on Darth Vader's giant cruiser... Vrad Dodonna takes Luke to a nearby planetoid.

HERE'S WHERE WE PART *COMPANY*, SKYWALKER!

THIS PLANETOID HAS ATMOSPHERE, SKYWALKER. UNTIL SOMEONE FINDS YOU...YOU CAN SURVIVE.

BUT THE *ALLIANCE* WON'T IF YOU DO THIS, VRAD.

IT'S DEAD *ANYWAY!* I REALIZED THAT THE *FIRST* TIME I FACED DARTH VADER'S NEW BATTLE CRUISER!

THEN WHY DID YOU *REJOIN* US?

ONCE THE EMPIRE *WINS*...THERE'LL BE *NO PLACE* AN EX-REBEL CAN HIDE. I NEEDED *SOMETHING* TO BARGAIN WITH.

T-THE... *POWER GEM!*

THE POWER GEM'S ONLY GOOD FOR ONE MORE *USE*, VRAD! THANKS TO YOU...IT MAY *ALREADY* BE EXHAUSTED!

THE EMPIRE DOESN'T *KNOW* THAT.

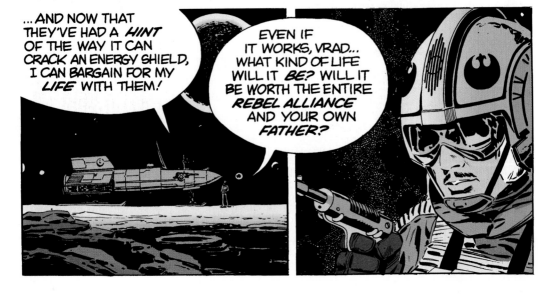

...AND NOW THAT THEY'VE HAD A *HINT* OF THE WAY IT CAN CRACK AN ENERGY SHIELD, I CAN BARGAIN FOR MY *LIFE* WITH THEM!

EVEN IF IT WORKS, VRAD... WHAT KIND OF LIFE WILL IT *BE*? WILL IT BE WORTH THE ENTIRE *REBEL ALLIANCE* AND YOUR OWN *FATHER*?

YOU CAN AFFORD TO BE SELF-RIGHTEOUS, SKYWALKER...YOU'VE GOT THE *FORCE* WITH YOU. ALL I EVER HAD WAS BEING *GENERAL DODONNA'S* SON!

AND FACING DARTH VADER'S CRUISER...THAT WASN'T *ENOUGH* ANYMORE!

THE POWER GEM ISN'T *TOTALLY* EXHAUSTED... WE COULD *STILL* MAKE ANOTHER STAB AT OUR MISSION!

VADER'S MONSTROSITY IS TOO FAR ALONG TOWARD *REBEL HEADQUARTERS* BY NOW...

...QUIT TRYING TO MAKE ME TURN BACK INTO A *HERO!* I'M USING THE *POWER GEM* TO BUY A SAFE EXISTENCE FROM THE EMPIRE!

VRAD!

Meanwhile...

LORD VADER...OUR BATTLE SCHEDULE DOESN'T *ALLOW* FOR REVERSING OUR *COURSE* LIKE THIS!

I SENSED THE *FORCE* ON THAT TINY REBEL SHIP... IT *MUST* BE LUKE SKYWALKER!

HE MUST HAVE SENSED THE *FORCE* WHEN WE FIRST ATTACKED HIS SHIP! THE MASS OF PLANETOIDS IN THIS SYSTEM WILL *CONFUSE* THEIR SCANNERS...

I-IT *CAN'T* BE! THAT MONSTER HAD A CLEAR COURSE TO OUR *MAIN BASE!* WHY WOULD VADER *TURN BACK?!*

FOR *ME.*

...BUT NOT FOR LONG! WE'VE GOT A *SECOND CHANCE*...LET'S *USE* IT!

YOU MUST BE A REAL *THREAT* TO THE EMPIRE FOR VADER'S SHIP TO *RETURN* LIKE THIS, SKYWALKER.

WE CAN *STRIKE* BEFORE HE FINDS ME, VRAD!

WHAT IF THE POWER GEM'S *TOO WEAK* NOW TO CRACK THEIR SHIELD? OR WE CAN'T HIT A VITAL SPOT IF WE *DO* CRACK IT?

TOO MANY *IFs*, SKYWALKER! YOU'RE BETTER OFF *HERE*...AND I'VE GOT MY *OWN* COURSE TO FOLLOW!

BETTER SHUT OFF THE HELMET COMLINK.

I *WON'T* LISTEN TO YOU...BUT THE *IMPERIALS* MIGHT TUNE IN!

And...

LORD VADER...LOOK AT *THIS!*

THERE, LORD VADER! THE REBEL SHIP THAT *ATTACKED* US... IT WAS HIDING ON A PLANETOID!

AFTER IT! I FELT THE *FORCE* EARLIER,... LUKE SKYWALKER *MUST* BE ABOARD!

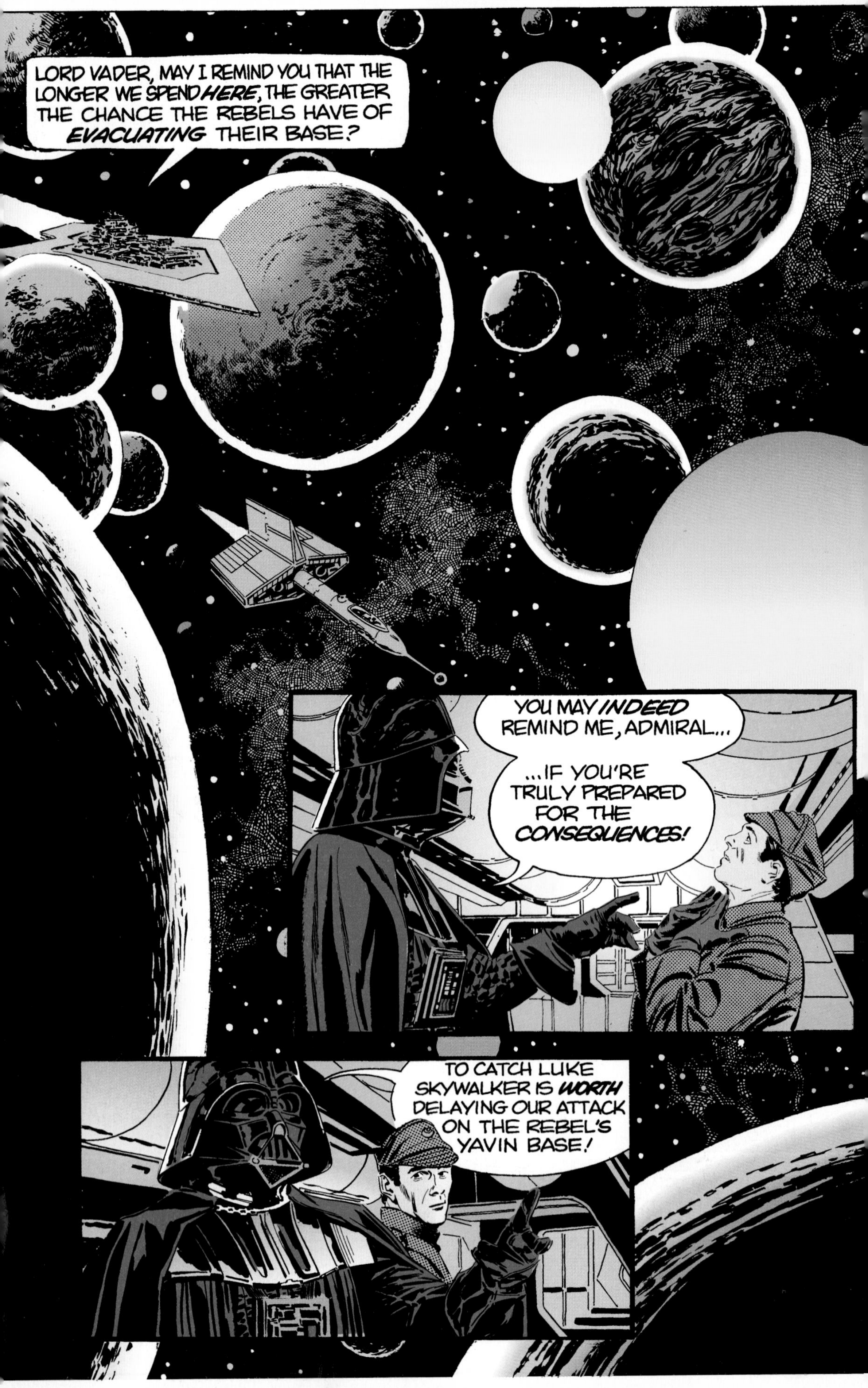
LORD VADER, MAY I REMIND YOU THAT THE LONGER WE SPEND *HERE*, THE GREATER THE CHANCE THE REBELS HAVE OF *EVACUATING* THEIR BASE?
YOU MAY *INDEED* REMIND ME, ADMIRAL...
...IF YOU'RE TRULY PREPARED FOR THE *CONSEQUENCES!*
TO CATCH LUKE SKYWALKER IS *WORTH* DELAYING OUR ATTACK ON THE REBEL'S YAVIN BASE!

NO! VRAD'S NOT ONLY RUN OUT ON ME AND THE MISSION...

...HE'S ATTRACTED DARTH VADER'S CRUISER RIGHT TO HIM!

I THOUGHT I'D REACHED VRAD ABOUT RESUMING THE MISSION WHEN DARTH VADER'S CRUISER RETURNED.

HE KIND OF LEFT YOU STRANDED, DIDN'T HE, KID? LUCKY YOU HAVE FRIENDS CONSIDERABLY LESS TRUSTING THAN YOU ARE!

NEXT TIME, KID, LISTEN TO ME ABOUT NOT VOLUNTEERING!

HAN...IS IT REALLY YOU? I THOUGHT I WAS STUCK ON THIS PLANETOID!

AT LEAST THE GENERAL'S SON IS PAYIN' NOW FOR LEAVIN' YOU!

But... THE REBEL CRAFT IS WITHIN *FIRING RANGE*, LORD VADER!

NO!

UNDER NO CIRCUMSTANCES ARE YOU TO *SHOOT* THE REBEL SHIP, ADMIRAL... WE'LL TAKE IT WITH OUR *TRACTOR BEAM!* I WANT LUKE SKYWALKER *UNHARMED!*

AND YET...IF HE'S *ABOARD,* WHY DON'T I FEEL THE *FORCE* AS I DID EARLIER WHEN THEY *FIRST* ATTACKED US?

I THOUGHT I'D *REACHED* VRAD DODONNA, HAN... CONVINCED HIM TO *FULFILL* OUR MISSION!

SURE, KID... THAT'S WHY HE *DITCHED* YOU ON THIS PLANETOID!

I OWED IT TO HIS *FATHER,* THE GENERAL. BESIDES, VRAD SEEMED ABOUT TO --

C'MON, KID! HE'S THINKIN' OF *HIMSELF* NOW...

...HOW LIKELY IS SOMEONE LIKE *THAT* TO CHANGE?

IT'S *STRANGE*, LORD VADER! THE REBEL CRAFT SHOULD BE TRYING TO JUMP TO *HYPERSPACE*!

SILENCE! I'M REACHING OUT WITH THE *FORCE* TO--

LORD VADER! IT'S CHANGED COURSE! IT'S *ATTACKING!*

WAROWWRRR!

THAT CAN'T *BE*, CHEWIE! LUKE, ACCORDIN' TO OUR SCOPES, VRAD DODONNA *DIDN'T* HIGHTAIL IT OUT OF THIS SYSTEM! IN FACT...

THE REBEL SHIP IS ATTACKING *HEAD ON*, LORD VADER!

THE POWER GEM *NEARLY* PENETRATED OUR SHIELDS. WE *MUST* DESTROY IT *NOW!*

ONCE *INSIDE* OUR SHIELD, EVEN *THAT* TINY SHIP MIGHT DO DAMAGE ENOUGH TO *RUIN* OUR MISSION, LORD VADER! LET ME TAKE *ACTION!*

NOT UNTIL I'M CERTAIN *LUKE SKYWALKER* IS NO LONGER ON THAT CRAFT, ADMIRAL. AT *THIS* RANGE, THE FORCE SHOULD CONFIRM...

"...THERE'S *NO TRACE* OF HIM!"

WE'VE GOT TO *TURN BACK*, HAN! IF VRAD DODONNA'S *ATTACKING* DARTH VADER'S CRUISER... IT MEANS HE *DID* LISTEN TO ME.

THEN WHY DID HE *ABANDON* YOU, LUKE?

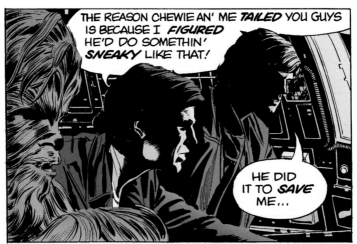

THE REASON CHEWIE AN' ME *TAILED* YOU GUYS IS BECAUSE I *FIGURED* HE'D DO SOMETHIN' *SNEAKY* LIKE THAT!

HE DID IT TO *SAVE* ME...

...THE POWER GEM MAY BE *TOO WEAK* NOW TO PENETRATE A DEFENSE SHIELD! IF IT *FAILS*...HE WANTED *ME* ALIVE TO CHALLENGE DARTH VADER SOME *OTHER* TIME!

WE'RE TRANSFERRING ALL SHIELDING *FORWARD*, LORD VADER! AGAINST *THAT*...EVEN THE MAD REBEL'S *POWER GEM* SHOULD FAIL!

And...

LUKE! LUKE?

HAN, THAT'S *VRAD* ON THE COMLINK...WE'VE *GOT* TO GO *BACK*!

KID...IT WON'T *HELP* HIM NOW! BUT...

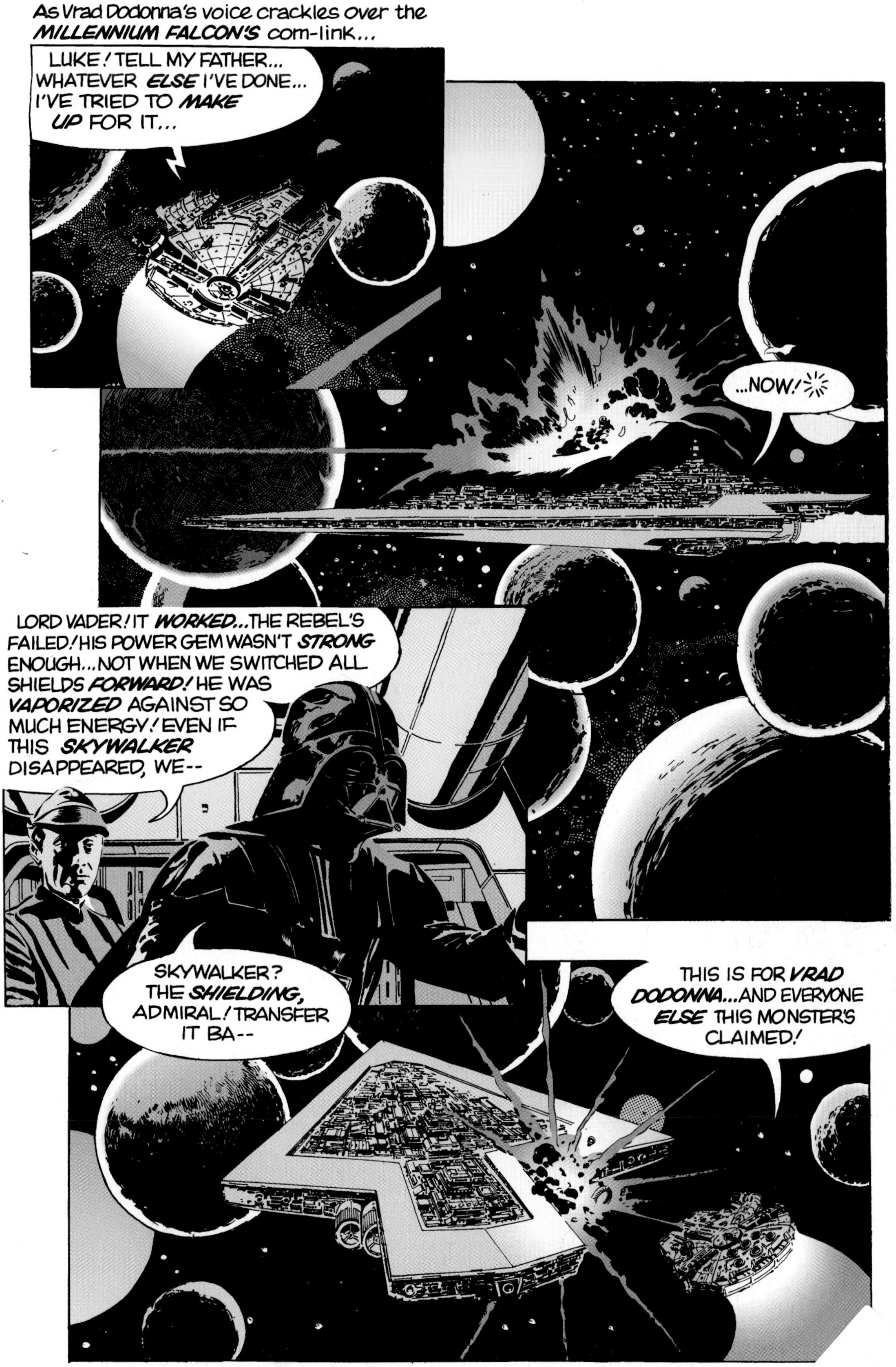
As Vrad Dodonna's voice crackles over the MILLENNIUM FALCON'S com-link...
LUKE! TELL MY FATHER... WHATEVER ELSE I'VE DONE... I'VE TRIED TO MAKE UP FOR IT...
...NOW!
LORD VADER! IT WORKED... THE REBEL'S FAILED! HIS POWER GEM WASN'T STRONG ENOUGH... NOT WHEN WE SWITCHED ALL SHIELDS FORWARD! HE WAS VAPORIZED AGAINST SO MUCH ENERGY! EVEN IF THIS SKYWALKER DISAPPEARED, WE--
SKYWALKER? THE SHIELDING, ADMIRAL! TRANSFER IT BA--
THIS IS FOR VRAD DODONNA... AND EVERYONE ELSE THIS MONSTER'S CLAIMED!

ER... LORD VADER, SINCE I TRANSFERRED ALL *DEFENSE SHIELDING* FORWARD AGAINST THE *FIRST* REBEL ATTACKER... I FEAR WE SUFFERED SOME SMALL...AH... *DAMAGE* JUST NOW...

...TO OUR *GYRO-CONTROL SYSTEM!* N-NOTHING BEYOND REPAIR, BUT *UNTIL* THEN...

WE CAN'T *TURN* THE CRUISER TO GIVE *PURSUIT* OR RESUME OUR *ATTACK!*

GREAT *SHOOTIN'*, LUKE...WE ONLY HAD *ONE CRACK* AT VADER'S BEHEMOTH BEFORE THEIR *SHIELD* WENT BACK UP!

IF IT HADN'T BEEN FOR *VRAD DODONNA*...

...WE WOULDN'T HAVE HAD *ANY* CRACKS, HAN! I WOULDN'T WANT TO TELL GENERAL DODONNA ABOUT *ALL* HIS SON'S RECENT ACTIONS...

...BUT FORTUNATELY VRAD MADE HIS *LAST* GESTURE THE ONE THAT WILL COUNT THE *MOST!*

I-IT'S REMARKABLE THAT WITH TIME FOR ONLY ONE BRIEF SHOT...THE REBELS WERE ABLE TO HIT ONE OF OUR *FEW* VULNERABLE SPOTS, LORD VADER!

IS IT ADMIRAL?

THOSE WHO SERVED ON THE *DEATH STAR* MIGHT DISAGREE...IF THEY WERE STILL *ALIVE!*

The *MILLENNIUM FALCON* returns to a Rebel headquarters under full evacuation...

GENERAL DODONNA'S WITH THE PRINCESS, KID...GONNA BE ROUGH *EXPLAINING* EVERYTHING ABOUT HIS SON!

I'LL STICK TO THE *IMPORTANT* THING, HAN...

"DESPITE THE POWER GEM FAILING, HE WENT AT THE ENEMY ANYWAY...SACRIFICING *HIMSELF,* FORCING THEM TO SWITCH ALL SHIELDS *FORWARD...*

"...LEAVING THEM VULNERABLE TO *US*, STRIKING FROM BEHIND!"

IF THE REBEL ALLIANCE ESCAPES TO THE *HOTH SYSTEM*...VRAD DODONNA DID HIS *PART!* THAT WON'T MAKE UP FOR THE GENERAL LOSING HIS SON...BUT MAYBE IT WILL *HELP!*

A FEW MORE *HOURS*, LORD VADER... THE REPAIRS WILL BE *COMPLETED!* WE CAN RESUME OUR *ATTACK--*

TOO *LATE* TO HALT THE REBEL EXODUS! BUT THE IMPERIAL FLEET MAINTAINING OUR BLOCKADE OF THE REBEL SECTOR *CAN!* CONTACT *ADMIRAL GRIFF!*

JOVAN STATION! Command center for the Imperial Blockade...

ADMIRAL GRIFF! ADMIRAL GRIFF!

I LEFT STRICT ORDERS **NOT** TO BE DISTURBED!

BUT **SIR!** IT'S **LORD VADER!**

THE REBELS HAVE SOMEHOW **STOPPED** HIS NEW BATTLE CRUISER, THE **EXECUTOR!**

THE **EXECUTOR** HAS BEEN STOPPED?! YOU'RE **LYING!**

THE REBELS WOULD NEED A **FLEET** TO DO THAT! THEY HAVEN'T ANY TO SPARE!

I-IT'S **TRUE,** ADMIRAL GRIFF! I DON'T KNOW THE DETAILS, BUT **LORD VADER** HIMSELF CONFIRMS IT!

HE'S **CALLING** YOU, SIR! I H-HOPE THIS **DISASTER** DOESN'T MEAN--

DISASTER? IT'S A **MIRACLE!**

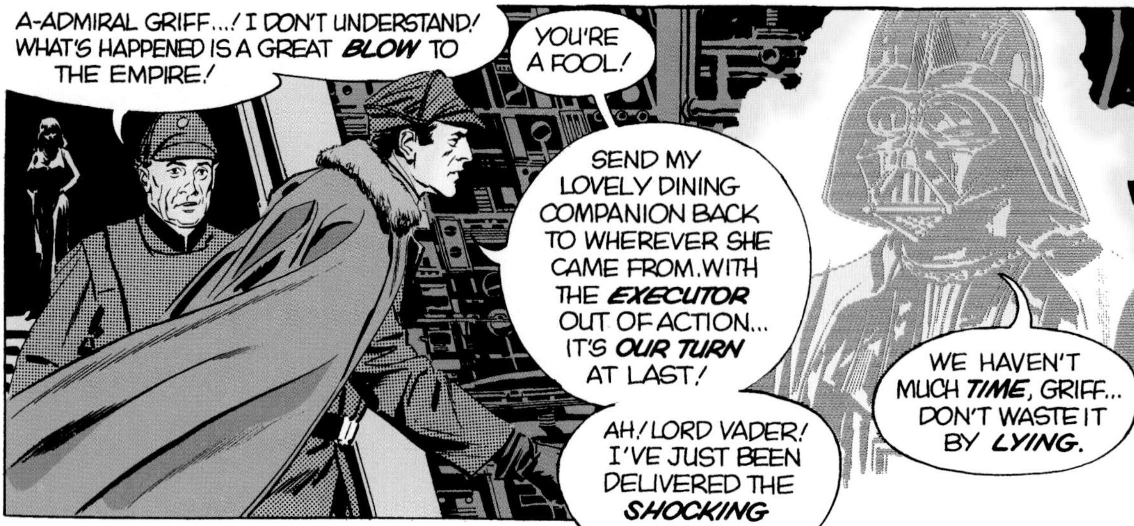
A-ADMIRAL GRIFF...! I DON'T UNDERSTAND! WHAT'S HAPPENED IS A GREAT BLOW TO THE EMPIRE!
YOU'RE A FOOL!
SEND MY LOVELY DINING COMPANION BACK TO WHEREVER SHE CAME FROM. WITH THE EXECUTOR OUT OF ACTION... IT'S OUR TURN AT LAST!
AH! LORD VADER! I'VE JUST BEEN DELIVERED THE SHOCKING NEWS!
WE HAVEN'T MUCH TIME, GRIFF... DON'T WASTE IT BY LYING.

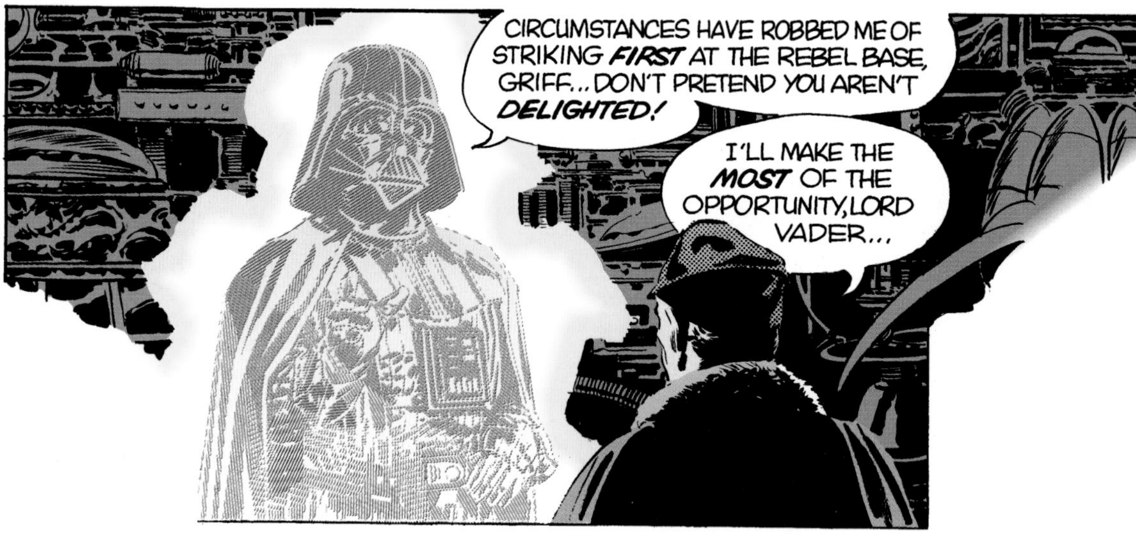
CIRCUMSTANCES HAVE ROBBED ME OF STRIKING FIRST AT THE REBEL BASE, GRIFF... DON'T PRETEND YOU AREN'T DELIGHTED!
I'LL MAKE THE MOST OF THE OPPORTUNITY, LORD VADER...

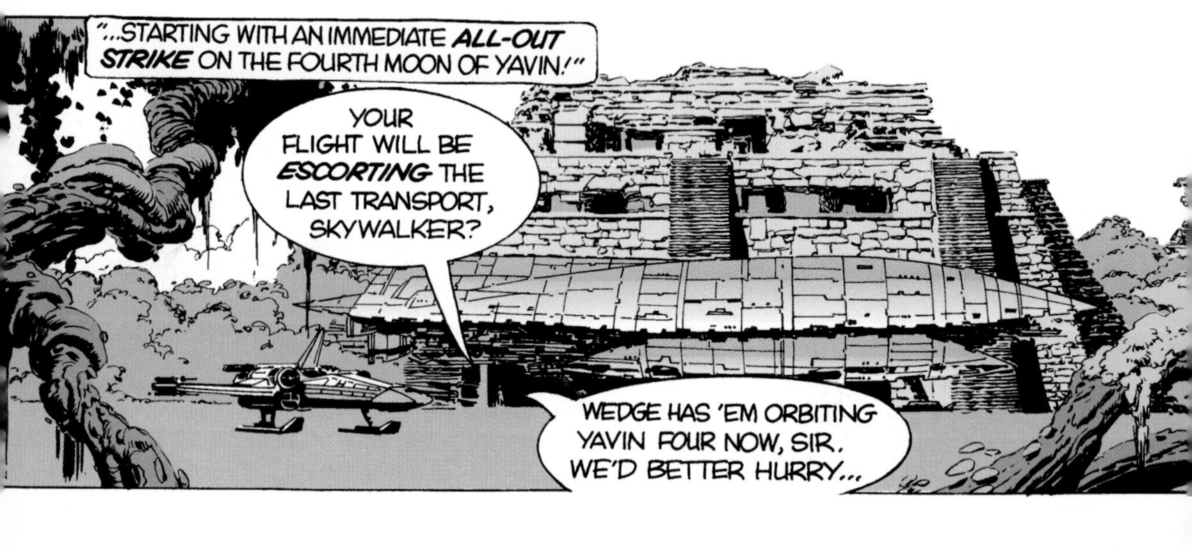
"...STARTING WITH AN IMMEDIATE ALL-OUT STRIKE ON THE FOURTH MOON OF YAVIN!"
YOUR FLIGHT WILL BE ESCORTING THE LAST TRANSPORT, SKYWALKER?
WEDGE HAS 'EM ORBITING YAVIN FOUR NOW, SIR. WE'D BETTER HURRY...

...THEY'LL BE EXPECTING US UP SOON, GENERAL DODONNA.

THERE'S ONE MORE *DUTY* TO PERFORM, MY BOY.

SHOULDN'T IT *WAIT* UNTIL WE RENDEZVOUS WITH THE OTHERS?

YOU FIRST JOINED US *HERE*, MY BOY...

...IT SEEMS ONLY FITTING THAT YAVIN FOUR BE WHERE YOU GET YOUR PROMOTION... *COMMANDER* SKYWALKER!

THERE'LL BE A MORE *FORMAL* CEREMONY WHEN YOU REJOIN THE PRINCESS AND YOUR FRIENDS AT THE RENDEZVOUS, SKYWALKER... BUT I WANTED TO MAKE IT OFFICIAL.

I'LL TRY TO BE *WORTHY* OF THE HONOR, GENERAL DODONNA!

IT'S LONG *OVERDUE*, MY BOY! AND WITH THE RECENT DEATH OF MY *SON*, THERE'S A VACANCY IN THE RANK. SO WHO BETTER TO... TO...

GENERAL?

Meanwhile, at Jovan Station...

THE REBELS WILL *PAY* FOR DAMAGING YOUR CRUISER, LORD VADER! I'M LAUNCHING A STRIKE FORCE TO *RAZE* THEIR BASE!

TO YOUR *SHIP*, COMMANDER SKYWALKER! I'VE DELAYED US ENOUGH!

AN OLD WAR-HORSE LIKE ME SHOULD KNOW HOW TO *DEAL* WITH THE DEATH OF A LOVED ONE!

WHERE'S THAT LAST *TRANSPORT* WE'RE ESCORTING, LUKE? SCANNERS INDICATE A WHOLE *FLOCK* OF HOSTILES ON THE WAY!

SHOULD BE RIGHT *BEHIND* ME, WEDGE! GENERAL DODONNA PULLED A SORT OF...UH...LAST-MINUTE *SURPRISE* THAT DELAYED US!

JUDGING BY THE *SCANNERS*... WE'RE CUTTING IT *CLOSE*, WEDGE!

THOSE IMPERIALS ARE *EAGER*, LUKE! LUCKY ALL THAT'S *WAITING* FOR 'EM IS AN *EMPTY BASE!*

HERE THEY ARE...LET'S *MOVE!* STOPPING DARTH VADER'S MONSTER CRUISER OBVIOUSLY DIDN'T DELAY THE *REST* OF THE IMPERIALS AS MUCH AS WE HOPED!

UH... COMMANDER SKYWALKER? THIS IS THE *TRANSPORT!* WE'VE JUST *CHECKED,* SIR... GENERAL DODONNA DOESN'T SEEM TO HAVE COME *ABOARD!*

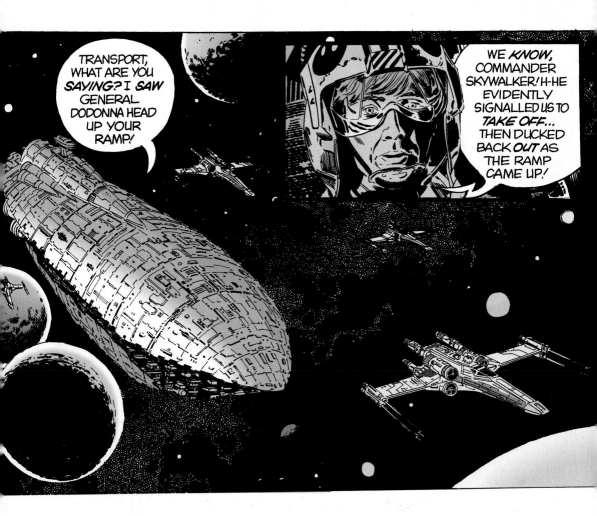

TRANSPORT, WHAT ARE YOU *SAYING?* I *SAW* GENERAL DODONNA HEAD UP YOUR RAMP!

WE *KNOW,* COMMANDER SKYWALKER! H-HE EVIDENTLY SIGNALLED US TO *TAKE OFF...* THEN DUCKED BACK *OUT* AS THE RAMP CAME UP!

As Imperial bombers dive on the base where he has stayed behind...General Dodonna speaks to Luke over the comlink.

YOU HAVE YOUR *ORDERS*, COMMANDER...

...GET THAT LAST TRANSPORT YOUR FLIGHT IS ESCORTING TO THE RENDEZVOUS *IMMEDIATELY!*

I'LL SEE THE EMPIRE DOESN'T *FOLLOW* YOU!

LUKE! WHAT'S GENERAL DODONNA *TALKING* ABOUT? WHAT'S HE GOING TO *DO?!*

FROM HIS REMARKS ABOUT HIS *HEALTH* FAILING SINCE THE DEATH OF HIS *SON,* WEDGE...

...I'M AFRAID HE'S CHOSEN TO *RETIRE*...IN A WAY THAT WILL TAKE THOSE IMPERIAL ATTACKERS *WITH* HIM!

General Dodonna ends his career with the Rebel Alliance in a *WARRIOR'S* way...

...and diving Imperial ships find their *TARGET* has become a devastating *TRAP!*

SOON, at Admiral Griff's Imperial Command Center...

...THE ENTIRE BOMBER FLEET *DESTROYED?* BLAST THOSE REBEL MADMEN!

BUT THEY STILL HAVEN'T ESCAPED OUR *BLOCKADE!* THEY'LL PAY *SOON...* AND *DEARLY!*

THE REBEL RENDEZVOUS! Luke's flight arrives with the last transport... and the news of General Dodonna's sacrifice.

WE HOPED THIS WOULD BE A *HAPPIER* OCCASION, KID...

BY SETTING OFF CONCUSSION CHARGES HE'D PLANTED ALL OVER THE MAIN BUILDINGS, HE GOT *THEM...*BUT SACRIFICED *HIMSELF.*

HE WENT OUT THE WAY AN OLD *WARRIOR* WOULD WANT TO, KID...AND WE'LL *HONOR* HIM BY GETTING THIS FLEET SAFELY TO *HOTH!*

AND THE *FIRST MOVE* IS UP TO OUR *MON CALAMARI* ALLIES!

A REPORT FROM *ADMIRAL GRIFF,* LORD VADER! THE REBELS HAVE SUCCESSFULLY *ABANDONED* THEIR YAVIN SYSTEM HEADQUARTERS.

BUT HAVE THEY ESCAPED THE *IMPERIAL BLOCKADE?*

RUSH *NOTHING.* I AM CONTENT TO TRUST THE ADMIRAL... FOR *NOW.*

NOT *YET,* SIR! I'LL *RUSH* OUR REPAIR EFFORTS SO YOU CAN TAKE *COMMAND* FROM GRIFF AND--

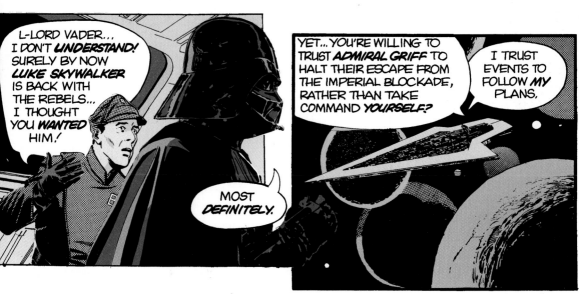

L-LORD VADER... I DON'T *UNDERSTAND!* SURELY BY NOW *LUKE SKYWALKER* IS BACK WITH THE REBELS... I THOUGHT YOU *WANTED* HIM!

MOST *DEFINITELY.*

YET... YOU'RE WILLING TO TRUST *ADMIRAL GRIFF* TO HALT THEIR ESCAPE FROM THE IMPERIAL BLOCKADE, RATHER THAN TAKE COMMAND *YOURSELF?*

I TRUST EVENTS TO FOLLOW *MY* PLANS.

READY MY *CRUISER!* TO ESCAPE OUR *BLOCKADE,* THE REBELS MUST MOVE *SOON*...I INTEND TO BE *WAITING* WHEN THEY DO!

YES, ADMIRAL GRIFF!

STILL *WAITIN',* YOUR ROYALNESS, THIS AIN'T *MY* IDEA OF HOW TO GET A *FLEET* PAST A BLOCKADE!

HAN, PERHAPS THAT'S WHY YOU'RE A *SMUGGLER*...INSTEAD OF A *GENERAL!* WE NEED A *DIVERSION* TO ESCAPE THE IMPERIALS AND THE *MON CALAMARI ALLIES* HAVE PROMISED--

PRINCESS! URGENT COMMUNICATION FROM *ADMIRAL ACKBAR!*

ADMIRAL ACKBAR'S MON CALAMARI FORCES HAVE HIT THE IMPERIALS AT VALLUSK CLUSTER!

TOO *OBVIOUS,* YOUR WORSHIP! THE IMPERIALS WILL *KNOW* IT'S A FEINT!

THEY'LL SIT *TIGHT!* THE MOMENT A CARAVAN *THIS* SIZE MOVES, EVERY SCANNER WILL LIGHT UP...

...AND THEIR BLOCKADE CAN CLOSE ON US LIKE A *FIST!*

OUR *FIRST* STRIKE HAS BEEN FOLLOWED BY *TWO MORE* AT OTHER POINTS ON THE IMPERIAL BLOCKADE!

STILL THINK THE DIVERSION IS TOO OBVIOUS, FLYBOY?

WE *MIGHT* JUST MAKE IT TO HOTH AFTER ALL, YOUR WORSHIP...

"...UNLESS THE EMPIRE'S MAN-IN-CHARGE IS REAL, REAL SHARP!"

ADMIRAL GRIFF! SOMETHING *UNEXPECTED*--

I'LL JUDGE THAT CAPTAIN...JUST SUPPLY THE FACTS.

AT FIRST, WE SUSPECTED A *FEINT*, ADMIRAL GRIFF... BUT THE BLOCKADE'S BEEN HIT AT THREE DIFFERENT POINTS. IT'S A *MAJOR ATTACK!*

AND BY THE *MON CALAMARI!*

WE DIDN'T KNOW THEY WERE *ALLIED* WITH THE REBELS! I'LL INFORM *LORD VADER* IMMEDIATELY, SIR!

LET HIM LEARN THROUGH *NORMAL* CHANNELS. I'LL HANDLE THIS *MYSELF!*

ADMIRAL GRIFF, IT SEEMS *DANGEROUS* TO PROCEED WITHOUT FULLY INFORMING LORD VADER!

HE PUT ME IN CHARGE OF THE BLOCKADE, CAPTAIN... IN RETURN FOR PAST FAVORS!

I WORKED IN HIS SHADOW FOR THE SAKE OF MY *CAREER*... NO LONGER!

TODAY, THE REBEL ESCAPE WILL BE *STOPPED*... THE REBELLION *CRUSHED!* BY *ME! ALONE!*

Imperial Admiral Griff turns from his aide... to intently study star chart displays for the sector he blockades.

BEFORE WE CAN STOP THE REBEL ESCAPE... THE MON CALAMARI MUST BE DEALT WITH! SHALL I TAKE ACTION?

SIR? SIR?!

THE MON CALAMARI ARE AN UNEXPECTED *DEVELOPMENT,* SIR... SURELY NOW YOU'LL *HAVE* TO TAKE COMMAND FROM ADMIRAL GRIFF!

I *HANDPICKED* THE ADMIRAL TO BE IN CHARGE OF OUR BLOCKADE...

...SURELY YOU DON'T *DOUBT* MY JUDGMENT? WE WILL *WAIT*... AND CONTINUE WITH REPAIRS... GRIFF IS AN *AMBITIOUS* MAN... I'M CERTAIN HE WON'T *DISAPPOINT* ME!

And...

ADMIRAL GRIFF! SHALL I DISPATCH SHIPS TO THE FORCES UNDER *ATTACK?*

NO! THE MON CALAMARI ARE OBVIOUSLY MEANT TO *DIVERT* US FROM THE *REAL* REBEL ESCAPE COURSE! BUT IT WON'T *WORK!*

THE REBELS CAN'T MOVE AN ENTIRE *FLEET* LIKE THEY DO THEIR BLASTED *BLOCKADE RUNNERS,* ADMIRAL GRIFF!

EXACTLY! TO GET THAT MANY SHIPS INTO HYPERSPACE...

...REQUIRES A LONG ESCAPE CORRIDOR. IF THEIR MON CALAMARI ALLIES ARE STRIKING AT *THIS* PART OF OUR BLOCKADE, THEN...

YES! I'VE *GOT* IT!

THE MON CALAMARI DIVERSION HAS LEFT A SMALL HOLE *UNCOVERED* IN OUR BLOCKADE NET! NO *IMPERIAL* FLEET WOULD CONSIDER USING IT...

...BUT A *SMALLER* FORCE LIKE THE REBELS HAVE MIGHT MAKE IT! *FULL SPEED...*

...WHEN THEY *TRY,* WE'LL BE THERE *WAITING!*

OUR MON CALAMARI ALLIES HAVE DONE *THEIR* PART... TIME FOR US TO *MOVE!* LUKE? READY TO TAKE *SCOUT POSITION?*

DOOTA-VRIP WHEEET!

ARTOO SAYS WE'RE *BOTH* READY, PRINCESS!

YOU'RE NOT LETTING THE KID SCOUT *ALONE* IN THAT SNUB FIGHTER? HE SHOULD AT LEAST HAVE THE *MILLENNIUM FALCON'S* FIREPOWER!

LUKE IS A REBEL *COMMANDER* NOW, HAN... HARDLY A *KID* ANYMORE.

YEAH, BUT IF *I* WAS RUNNIN' THIS SHOW--

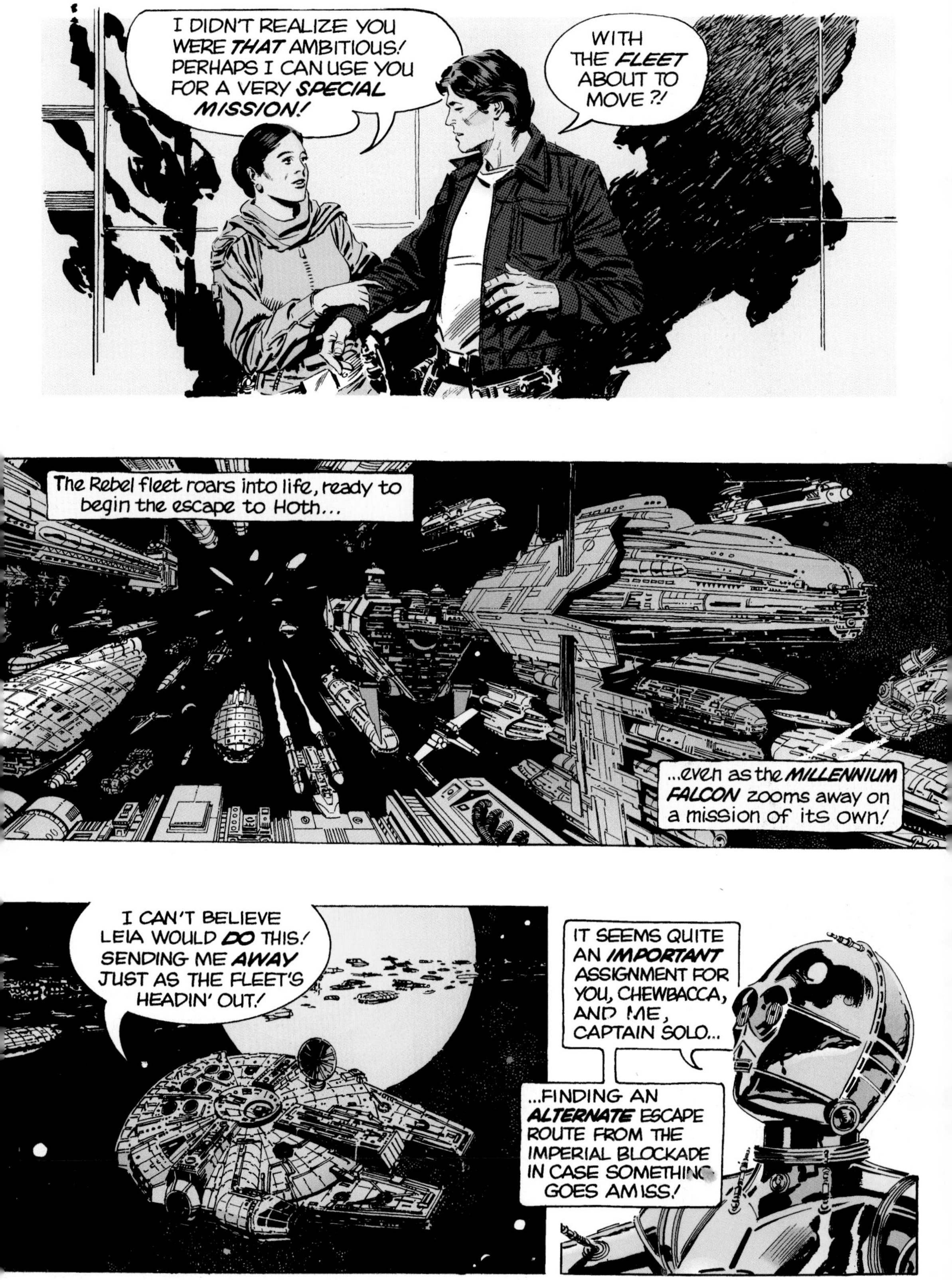
I DIDN'T REALIZE YOU WERE *THAT* AMBITIOUS! PERHAPS I CAN USE YOU FOR A VERY *SPECIAL MISSION!*
WITH THE *FLEET* ABOUT TO MOVE ?!
The Rebel fleet roars into life, ready to begin the escape to Hoth...
...even as the *MILLENNIUM FALCON* zooms away on a mission of its own!
I CAN'T BELIEVE LEIA WOULD *DO* THIS! SENDING ME *AWAY* JUST AS THE FLEET'S HEADIN' OUT!
IT SEEMS QUITE AN *IMPORTANT* ASSIGNMENT FOR YOU, CHEWBACCA, AND ME, CAPTAIN SOLO...
...FINDING AN *ALTERNATE* ESCAPE ROUTE FROM THE IMPERIAL BLOCKADE IN CASE SOMETHING GOES AMISS!

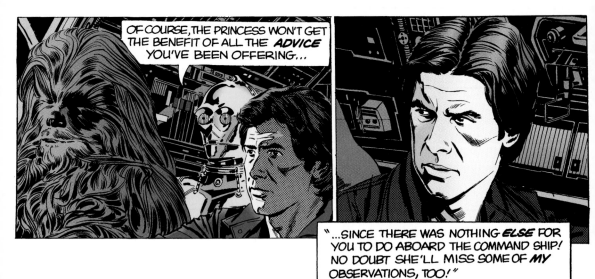

OF COURSE, THE PRINCESS WON'T GET THE BENEFIT OF ALL THE *ADVICE* YOU'VE BEEN OFFERING...

"...SINCE THERE WAS NOTHING *ELSE* FOR YOU TO DO ABOARD THE COMMAND SHIP! NO DOUBT SHE'LL MISS SOME OF *MY* OBSERVATIONS, TOO!"

Meanwhile...

THE LONG-RANGE SCANNERS HAVE DETECTED A LARGE AND SUDDEN EXPENDITURE OF *HEAT ENERGY*, ADMIRAL GRIFF! THE REBELS *MUST* BE MOVING...

RIGHT INTO MY *HANDS!*

And Luke scouts ahead for the Rebel escape fleet...

VA-DITTA TA BLEEP!

THE PRINCESS HAS SENT THEM TO LOOK FOR AN *ALTERNATE* COURSE?

IT'S ALWAYS GOOD TO HAVE A *BACK-UP*...BUT I BET THE *REAL* MISSION IS TO GET HAN OUT OF HER *HAIR!*

ADMIRAL GRIFF, PERHAPS *NOW* IS THE TIME TO INFORM LORD VADER WHAT WE--

HE'LL LEARN *AFTERWARD*...LIKE THE *REST* OF THE EMPIRE! THIS WILL BE *MY* TRIUMPH... *MINE ALONE!*

BEEDA-VRRRT!

THAT'S *RIGHT,* ARTOO... THE ENTIRE LENGTH OF THE FLEET'S ESCAPE CORRIDOR SEEMS *ALL CLEAR!*

A REBEL *SCOUT SHIP,* ADMIRAL GRIFF!

ITS INSTRUMENTS CAN'T *COMPARE* TO OURS. WE'RE CLOSE TO THE SUN...*HEAT DISTORTION* WILL PREVENT HIS SCANNERS DETECTING US.

Turning back...Luke suddenly dives toward the nearby sun!

IMPERIALS! COUNTING ON *HEAT DISTORTION* TO FOOL US, ARTOO... BUT NOT ON A *VISUAL CHECK!*

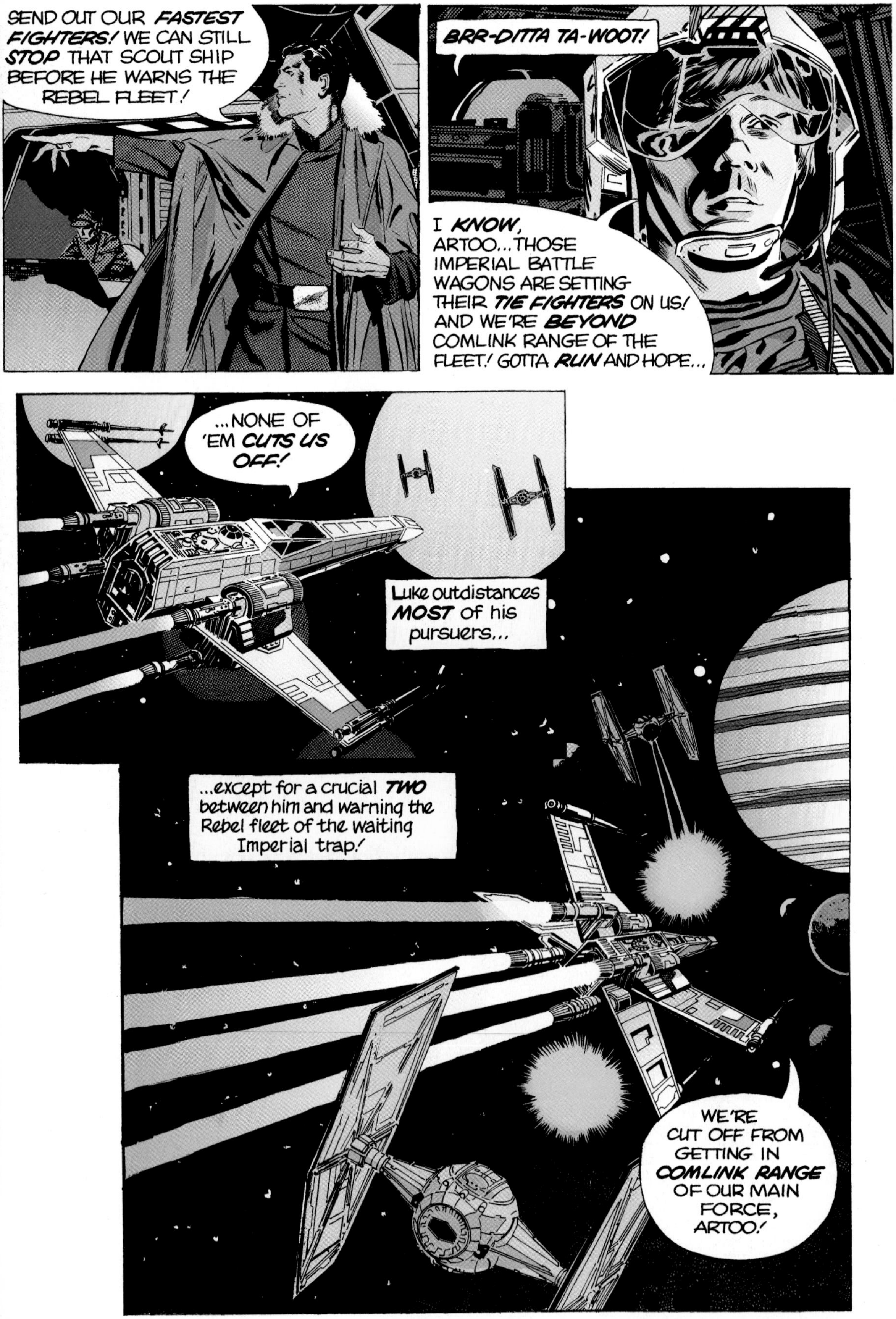
SEND OUT OUR FASTEST FIGHTERS! WE CAN STILL STOP THAT SCOUT SHIP BEFORE HE WARNS THE REBEL FLEET!
BRR-DITTA TA-WOOT!
I KNOW, ARTOO... THOSE IMPERIAL BATTLE WAGONS ARE SETTING THEIR TIE FIGHTERS ON US! AND WE'RE BEYOND COMLINK RANGE OF THE FLEET! GOTTA RUN AND HOPE...
...NONE OF 'EM CUTS US OFF!
Luke outdistances MOST of his pursuers...
...except for a crucial TWO between him and warning the Rebel fleet of the waiting Imperial trap!
WE'RE CUT OFF FROM GETTING IN COMLINK RANGE OF OUR MAIN FORCE, ARTOO!

AND IF THEY KEEP US IN THIS *CROSSFIRE*... WE WON'T *LAST* LONG ENOUGH TO EVER GET CLOSER!

GIVE ME *FULL STABILIZATION*, LITTLE GUY... I GOTTA TRY SOMETHING *DESPERATE!*

Meantime, the *MILLENNIUM FALCON* continues on *ITS* mission...

I DIDN'T THINK THERE *WAS* AN ALTERNATE ROUTE THE IMPERIALS WOULDN'T HAVE COVERED, CHEWIE! BUT THIS *LOOKS* LIKE--

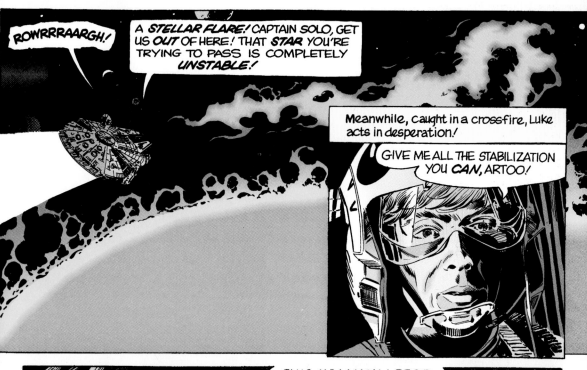

ROWRRRAARGH!

A *STELLAR FLARE!* CAPTAIN SOLO, GET US *OUT* OF HERE! THAT *STAR* YOU'RE TRYING TO PASS IS COMPLETELY *UNSTABLE!*

Meanwhile, caught in a crossfire, Luke acts in desperation!

GIVE ME ALL THE STABILIZATION YOU *CAN*, ARTOO!

PLUS ANY *LUCK* A DROID MIGHT HAVE PROGRAMMED INTO HIM!

One Imperial *TIE* fighter still on his tail, Luke rushes on a *COLLISION COURSE* toward the *OTHER* before him!

Then he hits full braking rockets and *DIVES* at the last possible instant!

MORE STABILIZATION, ARTOO! HOLD US *TOGETHER!*

Luke's wild maneuver costs him a *WING*, but his two *ENEMIES* suddenly find... their guns striking *EACH OTHER!* But...

WE'RE *BREAKING UP*, ARTOO! TRY TO HOLD US TOGETHER A FEW MORE MOMENTS! MAYBE WE'RE CLOSE ENOUGH *NOW* TO RAISE THE FLEET!

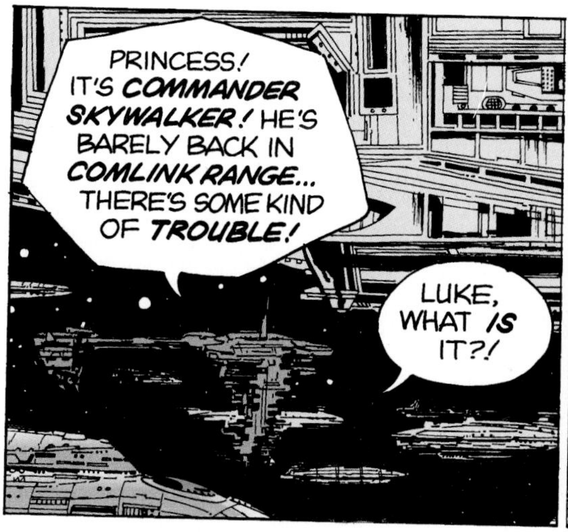
PRINCESS! IT'S COMMANDER SKYWALKER! HE'S BARELY BACK IN COMLINK RANGE... THERE'S SOME KIND OF TROUBLE!
LUKE, WHAT IS IT?!

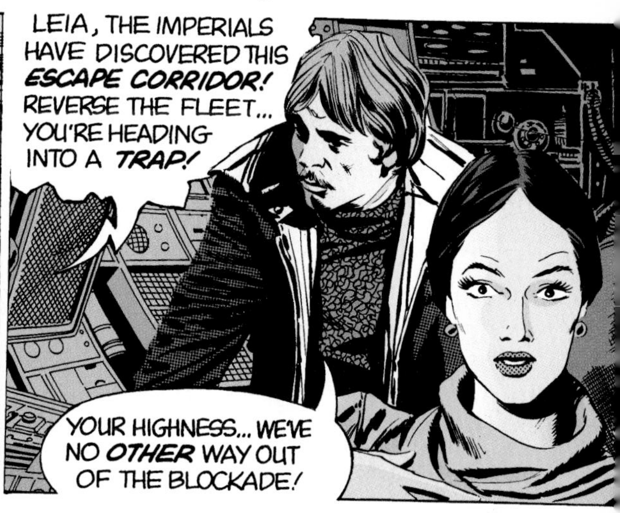
LEIA, THE IMPERIALS HAVE DISCOVERED THIS ESCAPE CORRIDOR! REVERSE THE FLEET... YOU'RE HEADING INTO A TRAP!
YOUR HIGHNESS... WE'VE NO OTHER WAY OUT OF THE BLOCKADE!

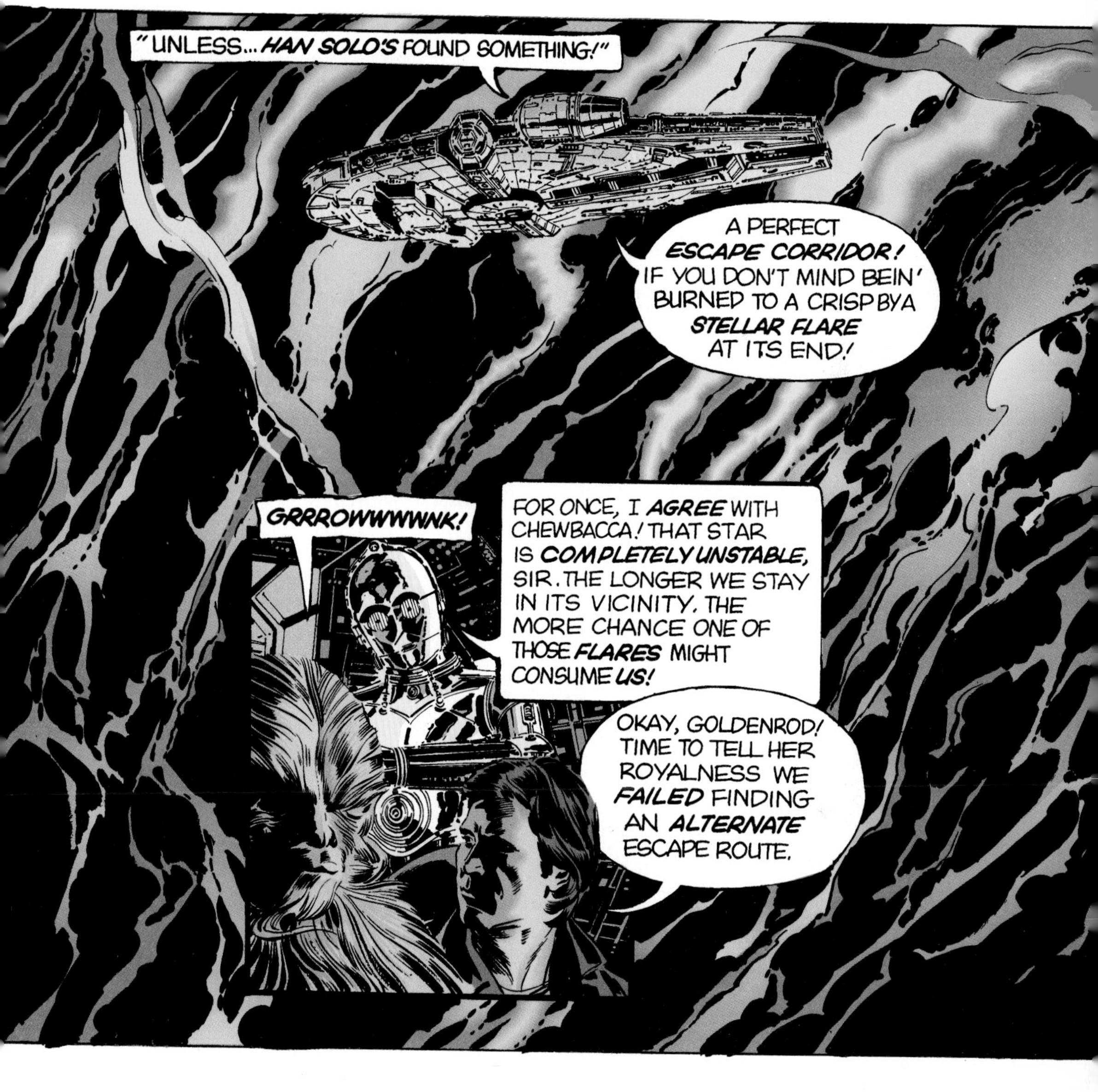
"UNLESS... HAN SOLO'S FOUND SOMETHING!"
A PERFECT ESCAPE CORRIDOR! IF YOU DON'T MIND BEIN' BURNED TO A CRISP BY A STELLAR FLARE AT ITS END!
GRRROWWWWNK!
FOR ONCE, I AGREE WITH CHEWBACCA! THAT STAR IS COMPLETELY UNSTABLE, SIR. THE LONGER WE STAY IN ITS VICINITY, THE MORE CHANCE ONE OF THOSE FLARES MIGHT CONSUME US!
OKAY, GOLDENROD! TIME TO TELL HER ROYALNESS WE FAILED FINDING AN ALTERNATE ESCAPE ROUTE.

Meanwhile, unknown to the *MILLENNIUM FALCON* crew...

ADMIRAL GRIFF! THE REBEL SCOUT *ESCAPED* THE CROSSFIRE HE WAS IN... CAUSED OUR FIGHTERS TO *DESTROY* EACH OTHER!

HIS OWN SHIP IS BREAKING UP, BUT HE GOT FAR ENOUGH TO *WARN* HIS FLEET OF OUR *TRAP!*

THEY HAVE NO *OTHER* ESCAPE CORRIDOR.../ *FULL SPEED!* WE CAN *STILL* CATCH THEM!

Leia informs the *MILLENNIUM FALCON* crew of Luke's last message!

SCATTER THE FLEET, YOUR WORSHIP... *SOME* SHIPS MIGHT ESCAPE! I'M GOIN' AFTER *LUKE!*

THAT *ALTERNATE* ESCAPE CORRIDOR YOU FOUND, HAN... PERHAPS WE CAN *BYPASS* THE OBSTACLE!

OBSTACLE? AN UNSTABLE *SUN*...ERUPTING WITH *STELLAR FLARES?!* DON'T EVEN *CONSIDER* IT!

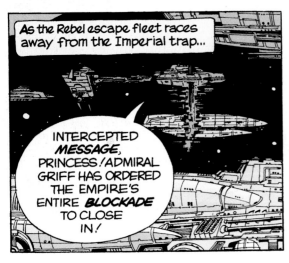

As the Rebel escape fleet races away from the Imperial trap...

INTERCEPTED *MESSAGE*, PRINCESS! ADMIRAL GRIFF HAS ORDERED THE EMPIRE'S ENTIRE *BLOCKADE* TO CLOSE IN!

SHOULD WE *SCATTER?* IT WILL MEAN MANY *LOSSES*, BUT...

THEN LET'S NOT *RUSH* TO GET THEM...

...ESPECIALLY IF IN THE MEANTIME HAN MIGHT FIND *LUKE!*

CAPTAIN SOLO, THE FLEET'S FINAL REPORT FROM MASTER LUKE INDICATED HIS SCOUT SHIP WAS *BREAKING UP!*

HE PROBABLY *JETTISONED,* GOLDENROD!

ONLY... BY MY CALCULATIONS... WE SHOULD'VE *SPOTTED* HIM BY NOW! AND--

SIR! *WRECKAGE* AHEAD! BUT... NO *TRACE* OF MASTER LUKE OR ARTOO!

On the *FAR* side of the X-Wing wreckage...

MASTER LUKE AND ARTOO... *HIDING!* SO THEY WOULDN'T BE DETECTED BY ENEMY SHIPS!

But once the **RESCUE** is made...

THE FLEET'S **HAD** IT, KID! SCATTERING'S THEIR ONLY CHANCE!

UNLESS THEY COULD **DODGE** THE STELLAR FLARE CUTTING OFF THAT **ROUTE** YOU FOUND...

LUKE, YOU SOUND JUST LIKE HER **ROYALNESS!** THERE'S NO **DODGING** A STELLAR FLARE! AND WITH AN UNSTABLE STAR...

...THERE'S NO **PREDICTIN'** WHEN ONE WILL ERUPT! I WISH I HADN'T TOLD **EITHER** OF YOU ABOUT THAT ROUTE...YOU'RE WASTIN' **ESCAPE** TIME **THINKIN'** ABOUT IT!

WE'RE ON OUR **OWN,** KID...LEIA **HAS** TO HAVE SCATTERED THE FLEET BY NOW.

IF SHE FOLLOWED YOUR **ADVICE,** CAPTAIN SOLO. BUT SINCE THE EXODUS FROM YAVIN, SHE HASN'T REALLY--

WHAT **ELSE** COULD SHE DO, BRIGHT EYES?

...TRY TO TAKE THE ENTIRE FLEET PAST THE **STELLAR FLARE**?!

INTERESTING YOU SHOULD **SAY** THAT, SIR. IT'S WHERE CHEWBACCA REPORTS OUR SHIPS ARE **CURRENTLY** HEADED!

As the Imperial blockade closes on the Rebel fleet...

WHERE'S *LORD VADER?* ALL *REPAIRS* ARE COMPLETED! WE CAN JOIN THE *ACTION* AT LAST!

ONLY IF YOU WISH TO RISK *DISTURBING* HIM IN HIS *MEDITATION POD!*

...WE COULD *JOIN* IN CRUSHING THE ALLIANCE! INSTEAD, *ADMIRAL GRIFF* HOGS THE GLORY... WHILE WE WASTE--

YOU *MISJUDGE* GRIFF'S ROLE AND MY MEDITATION... *FATALLY!*

L-LORD VADER! I THOUGHT YOU WERE *MEDITATING!* I FEARED--

THAT *ADMIRAL GRIFF* WOULD DESTROY THE REBEL ALLIANCE RATHER THAN *US!*

I'VE *USED* GRIFF... TO EXHAUST THE REBELS AND DRIVE THEM INTO *MY* HANDS!

B-BUT...WE'RE NOWHERE *NEAR* THEM... AND HAVE NO *NOTION* OF THEIR POSITION!

WE WILL LEARN *THAT* AND FAR *MORE*... BUT ONLY IF I AM NOT *FURTHER* DISTURBED BY COMPLAINING FOOLS!

FIND A *REPLACEMENT* FOR OUR DOUBTING FRIEND! AND WHEN *NEXT* I EMERGE FROM THE MEDITATION POD...

...HAVE THE SHIP READY TO MOVE *INSTANTLY!*

Meanwhile...

HAN...LEIA'S DOING THE *RIGHT THING!*

KID, I WROTE THE BOOK ON GALACTIC *RISK-TAKING* AND LEADING A FLEET PAST AN UNSTABLE STAR KICKIN' OUT *STELLAR FLARES* ISN'T *IN* IT!

WE GOTTA CATCH UP AND *STOP* HER!

NO, HAN! WE'VE GOT TO TAKE OVER THE *LEAD* FROM HER!

The *MILLENNIUM FALCON* overtakes the Rebel escape fleet...

LEIA SHOULD'VE *SCATTERED* 'EM WHILE SHE HAD THE CHANCE, LUKE!

HER *INSTINCTS* ARE CORRECT, HAN!

OUR SHIPS *COULD* GET PAST THOSE STELLAR FLARE ERUPTIONS...IF SOMEONE WERE ABLE TO SENSE WHEN IT WAS *SAFE* TO MOVE...

YEAH, BUT WHO--OH, *NO!*

LUKE, YOU'RE NOT THINKIN' WHAT I *THINK* YOU'RE THINKIN'...?!

GET US AS *CLOSE* TO THAT UNSTABLE STAR AS WE *DARE*, HAN *!*

Admiral Griff races after the Rebel fleet...

MORE *SPEED!* WE'RE TOO CLOSE TO *TRIUMPH* FOR ANY DELAY!

WE CAN'T DO BETTER AT *SUB-LIGHT,* SIR...

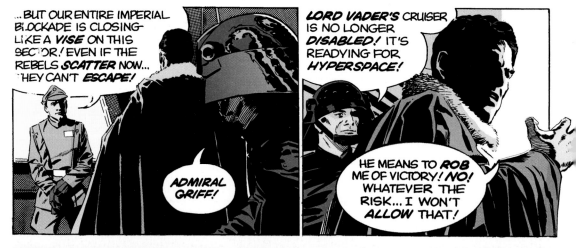

...BUT OUR ENTIRE IMPERIAL BLOCKADE IS CLOSING LIKE A *VISE* ON THIS SECTOR! EVEN IF THE REBELS *SCATTER* NOW... THEY CAN'T *ESCAPE!*

ADMIRAL GRIFF!

LORD VADER'S CRUISER IS NO LONGER *DISABLED!* IT'S READYING FOR *HYPERSPACE!*

HE MEANS TO *ROB* ME OF VICTORY! *NO!* WHATEVER THE RISK... I WON'T *ALLOW* THAT!

Meanwhile, the *MILLENNIUM FALCON* overtakes the fleet! And...

LUKE, HOW CAN WE *POSSIBLY* HELP THEM PAST THAT STELLAR-FIRE SPITTIN' NIGHTMARE?!

PERHAPS THE *FORCE* WILL BE WITH US! *CLOSER,* HAN!

KID, ANY CLOSER AND WE'LL *FRY*, EVEN IF THAT SUN *DOESN'T* SEND A STELLAR FLARE ERUPTING OUR WAY!

THEN... IT'S ALL UP TO *ME*.

KEEP A *COMLINK* OPEN TO LEIA AND THE FLEET, HAN...BUT SHUT DOWN ALL *OTHER* SYSTEMS.

LUKE, WHAT HAPPENS WHEN THE NEXT *STELLAR FLARE* ERUPTS?!

AN ERUPTION LIKE THAT HAS TO *BUILD*, HAN...AND IT'S POWERFUL ENOUGH TO CAUSE A *DISTURBANCE* IN THE *FORCE*...WITH NOTHING TO *DISTRACT* ME... I SHOULD *DETECT* IT!

KID, WE'RE GAMBLIN' ON YOU BEING ABLE TO *DETECT* A STELLAR FLARE BUILDIN'... BY CONCENTRATING ON THE *FORCE?*

I'M NOT *BEN KENOBI*, HAN...

...BUT WITH A DISTURBANCE OF *THAT* MAGNITUDE, I SHOULD BE ABLE TO *SENSE* IT COMING!

In the unusual quiet of the shut-down *MILLENNIUM FALCON*, Luke sits alone...reaching out with his feelings...

...concentrating on the unstable *STAR* beyond...

...and unknowingly *BETRAYING* himself!

YES! I KNEW IF ADMIRAL GRIFF PUSHED YOUR REBEL FRIENDS *HARD* ENOUGH, YOUNG SKYWALKER... YOU'D TRY *AIDING* THEM WITH THE *FORCE!*

HAN...I SENSE *CALM*...NO DISTURBANCE IN THE *FORCE* YET FROM THAT SUN...TELL LEIA TO SEND PART OF THE *FLEET* THROUGH!

ADMIRAL GRIFF! THE REBELS SEEM ABOUT TO TRY A... *SUICIDE MANEUVER!*

NO! I WON'T BE *ROBBED* OF VICTORY! LEAP TO *HYPERSPACE!*

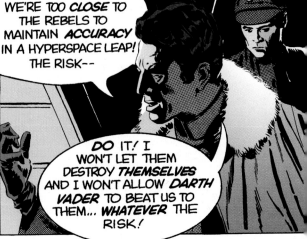

WE'RE TOO *CLOSE* TO THE REBELS TO MAINTAIN *ACCURACY* IN A HYPERSPACE LEAP! THE RISK--

DO IT! I WON'T LET THEM DESTROY *THEMSELVES* AND I WON'T ALLOW *DARTH VADER* TO BEAT US TO THEM... *WHATEVER* THE RISK!

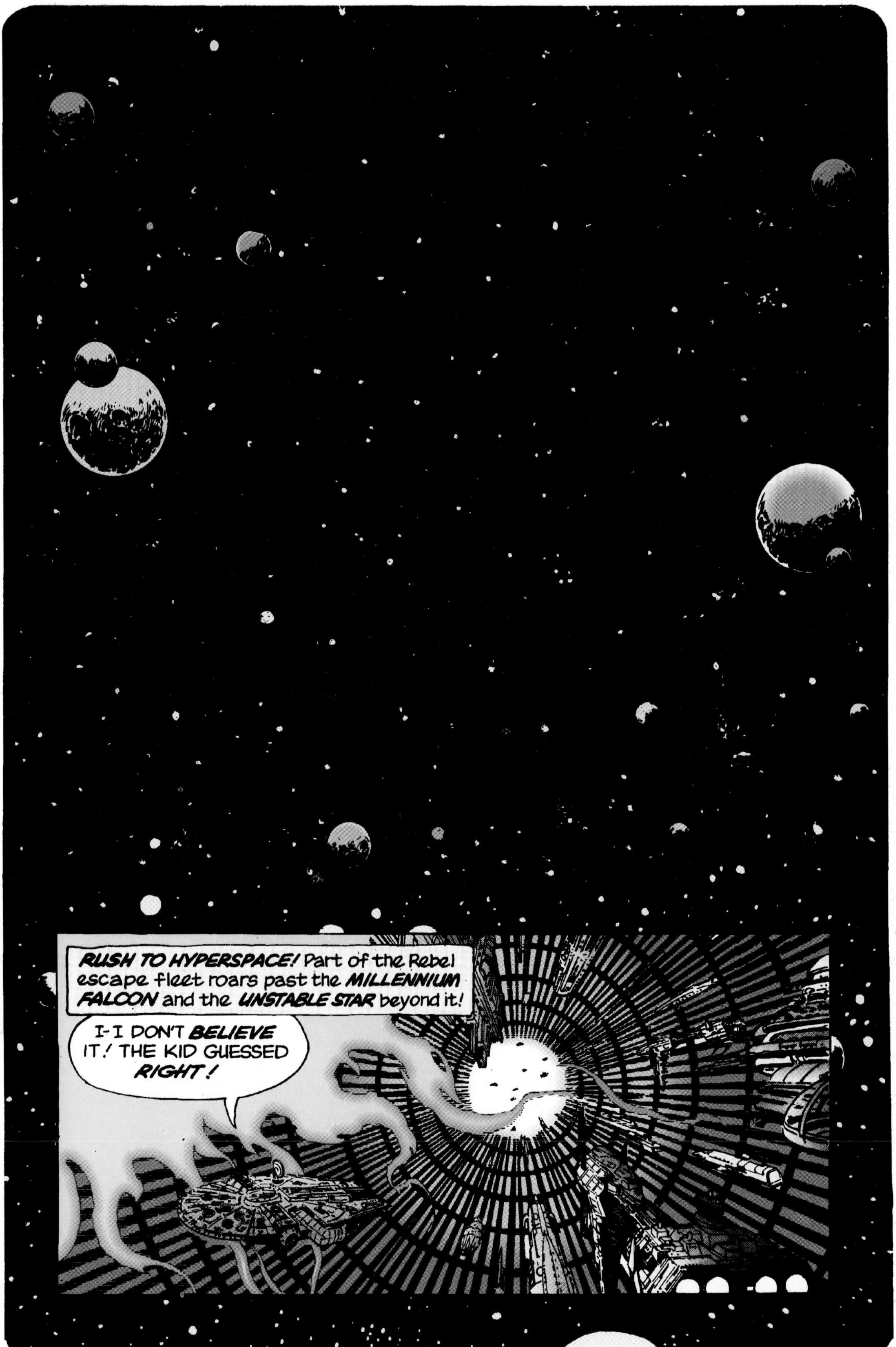
RUSH TO HYPERSPACE! Part of the Rebel escape fleet roars past the MILLENNIUM FALCON and the UNSTABLE STAR beyond it!
I-I DON'T BELIEVE IT! THE KID GUESSED RIGHT!

IT'S QUITE *LOGICAL*, CAPTAIN SOLO! THE TREMENDOUS POWER OF A *STELLAR FLARE* BUILDING TO ERUPT CREATES A DISTURBANCE IN THE *FORCE*...AND MASTER LUKE CAN *SENSE* THAT!

THERE'S *NOTHIN'* LOGICAL ABOUT MUMBO JUMBO LIKE THE *FORCE*, BRIGHT EYES!

HAN! THREEPIO... *PLEASE!* I'M *NOT* BEN KENOBI... I NEED QUIET...FULL CONCENTRATION FOR THIS!

But as a *RESULT* of that concentration...

FULL SPEED! LUKE SKYWALKER HAS *REVEALED* HIMSELF TO ME!

YES, LORD VADER! BUT *ADMIRAL GRIFF* IS DOING EVERYTHING TO REACH THE REBELS *FIRST!*

Aware the Alliance fleet is getting away, Admiral Griff orders his pursuing cruisers into hyperspace!

SIR, IF WE MISCALCULATE EVEN *SLIGHTLY*...

...WE'LL COME OUT IN THE *CENTER* OF THAT *SUN* THE REBELS ARE PASSING!

THEY'RE RISKING ITS *STELLAR FLARE ERUPTIONS!* WE'LL WIN BY *MATCHING* THEIR BOLDNESS!

WE'VE LOST *SOME* OF THE REBEL FLEET ALREADY, ADMIRAL GRIFF!

BUT BY COMING OUT OF HYPERSPACE ON THE *FAR SIDE* OF THAT UNSTABLE SUN...

...WE CAN STILL CATCH *MOST* OF THEM... JUST AS THEY'RE BUILDING SPEED FOR THEIR FINAL *LEAP* TO FREEDOM!

Unaware of Admiral Griff's desperate move to overtake the Rebel fleet...Luke continues to guide them past the unstable sun...

...by reaching out with the *FORCE!*

HAN! TELL LEIA TO HALT ALL *SHIPS!* SOMETHING'S ABOUT TO HAPPEN... SOMETHING *BAD!*

Barely has Han given word to *HALT* the Rebel fleet's passage than...

STELLAR FLARE! KICKIN' OUT RIGHT WHERE OUR *SHIPS* WOULD'VE BEEN!

MASTER LUKE'S DOING A *MAGNIFICENT* JOB...USING THE FORCE TO *SENSE* EACH DISTURBANCE BUILDING!

QUIET, BRIGHT EYES! DON'T SHATTER HIS CONCENTRATION...SOMETHIN' MIGHT BE ERUPTIN' *OUR* WAY!

ANOTHER STELLAR FLARE! IF THAT MISERABLE FIREBALL KEEPS HICCUPIN'...THE REST OF THE FLEET'LL *NEVER* GET PAST!

H-HAN? I THINK I PERCEIVE A *PATTERN!*

What Luke *DOESN'T* perceive is that his use of the Force draws another...

THE REBELS ARE TRULY *MAD,* LORD VADER! HOW CAN THEY TAKE THEIR FLEET PAST AN *UNSTABLE SUN?*

WITH THE *FORCE,* ANYTHING IS POSSIBLE...

...AND *ONE* AMONG THEM-- THOUGH YET UNTRAINED-- IS *STRONG* WITH IT! FORTUNATELY, HE WILL *NOT* BE WITH THEM MUCH LONGER!

From the *MILLENNIUM FALCON*, word goes out to the remainder of the Rebel fleet...

LUKE SAYS TAKE 'EM *THROUGH*, PRINCESS!

BUT, *HAN*...

"...OUR INSTRUMENTS INDICATE *STELLAR FLARES* ARE CURRENTLY ERUPTING FROM THAT UNSTABLE SUN!"

"YOU DON'T HAVE TO TELL *ME*, YOUR ROYALNESS... WE'RE CLOSER THAN *ANYBODY!*"

ACCORDING TO LUKE'S SENSE OF THE DISTURBANCE IN THE FORCE...THEY'RE *RECEDING* IN STRENGTH! GO *NOW* AND THEY SHOULDN'T *TOUCH* YOU...

WAIT 'TIL THEY DIE...AND THE *EMPIRE* COULD ARRIVE!

And on the troublesome star's **FAR** side, the Empire **HAS**... in the form of Darth Vader's **EXECUTOR** dropping from hyperspace.

EXCELLENT! NEITHER THE REBELS **NOR** ADMIRAL GRIFF HAVE COME THROUGH!

The word goes out...move the rest of the fleet!

PRINCESS! IS COMMANDER SKYWALKER **SURE?** STELLAR FLARES ARE **STILL** ERUPTING FROM THAT UNSTABLE SUN!

LUKE'S READING OF THE FLARES' PATTERNS IS THAT THEY'RE **RECEDING** IN STRENGTH! WE CAN GO **NOW**--BEFORE THE **EMPIRE** ARRIVES--AND NOT BE TOUCHED!

I **HOPE!**

FULL SPEED TO THE **CENTER** OF THE SYSTEM! WE'LL CATCH YOUNG SKYWALKER AND HIS FRIENDS AS THEY COME THROUGH!

YOU'VE TRICKED **ADMIRAL GRIFF** INTO DRIVING THE PRIZE INTO **OUR** HANDS, LORD VADER!

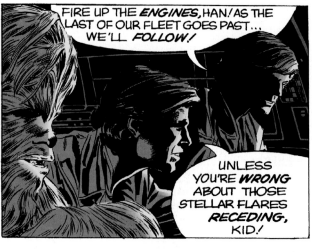

FIRE UP THE **ENGINES**, HAN! AS THE LAST OF OUR FLEET GOES PAST... WE'LL **FOLLOW!**

UNLESS YOU'RE **WRONG** ABOUT THOSE STELLAR FLARES **RECEDING**, KID!

The Rebel fleet soars past the dwindling stellar flares of the unstable sun...into *RANGE* of Darth Vader's waiting cruiser!

THE REBELS ARE MOVING *NOW,* LORD VADER... WE *HAVE* THEM!

AND *STILL* NO SIGN OF *ADMIRAL GRIFF?*

ALL GUNS *FIRE!*

Then...

SOMETHING'S *COLLIDED* WITH OUR FORCE FIELD!

Before the *EXECUTOR* can blast the Alliance fleet...

THREE OF OUR OWN *CRUISERS!* DROPPING OUT OF HYPERSPACE RIGHT *INTO* US, LORD VADER! WHAT--?

ADMIRAL GRIFF!

NO *DAMAGE,* LORD VADER... THANKS TO OUR SHIELD.' BUT THAT ZEALOUS FOOL, *ADMIRAL GRIFF,* WAS DESTROYED!

I USED HIS AMBITION TO DRIVE THE REBELS TO *ME...*

...I DIDN'T FORESEE IT WOULD ALSO DRIVE *HIM* TO THE MADNESS OF AN INACCURATE *HYPERSPACE LEAP* IN AN EFFORT TO *BEAT* US!

LORD VADER, ONCE WE SWING BACK INTO *FIRING POSITION,* WE CAN--

--WATCH THE *LAST* REBEL SHIP DISAPPEARING INTO HYPERSPACE.

SO ONCE MORE, YOUNG SKYWALKER, THE INEVITABLE IS *PROLONGED!* BUT THE DAY *CANNOT* BE AVOIDED WHEN YOU WILL FINALLY *FACE* ME...

...MY SON!

The *MILLENNIUM FALCON* darts for hyperspace... following the other Alliance ships past a suddenly *THWARTED* enemy!

KID, AM I CRAZY OR DID WE JUST GET HANDED A *MIRACLE!*

DARTH VADER'S CRUISER HAD OUR WHOLE FLEET *COLD* AS IT CAME AROUND THAT UNSTABLE SUN!

YAHOO! *HOTH*...HERE WE COME!

The *HOTH* system...

WE'LL SOON BE AT OUR NEW BASE, PRINCESS LEIA!

THE *MILLENNIUM FALCON* TRAILED THE FLEET THROUGH HYPERSPACE... IS IT ALL RIGHT?

COMMANDER SKYWALKER AND CAPTAIN SOLO WAITED TO BE CERTAIN THE REST OF OUR FLEET MADE IT INTO HYPERSPACE BEFORE FOLLOWING, PRINCESS. IT'LL *TAKE* THEM LONGER.

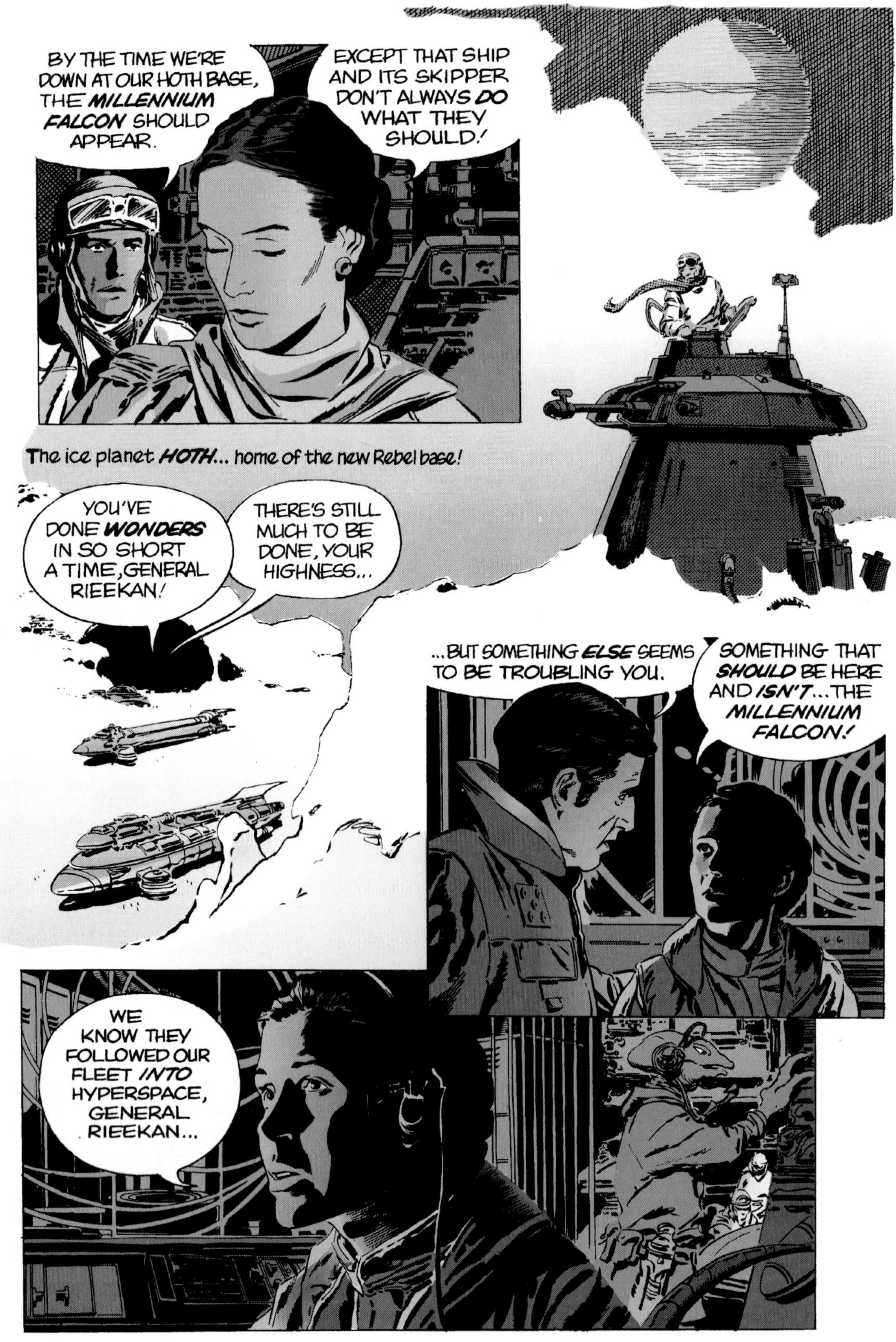
BY THE TIME WE'RE DOWN AT OUR HOTH BASE, THE *MILLENNIUM FALCON* SHOULD APPEAR.
EXCEPT THAT SHIP AND ITS SKIPPER DON'T ALWAYS *DO* WHAT THEY SHOULD!
The ice planet *HOTH*... home of the new Rebel base!
YOU'VE DONE *WONDERS* IN SO SHORT A TIME, GENERAL RIEEKAN!
THERE'S STILL MUCH TO BE DONE, YOUR HIGHNESS...
...BUT SOMETHING *ELSE* SEEMS TO BE TROUBLING YOU.
SOMETHING THAT *SHOULD* BE HERE AND *ISN'T*...THE *MILLENNIUM FALCON!*
WE KNOW THEY FOLLOWED OUR FLEET *INTO* HYPERSPACE, GENERAL RIEEKAN...

"...BUT WHY NOT *OUT?*"

ROW ROWWWK!

DON'T TELL *ME* I DON'T KNOW WHERE WE ARE, CHEWIE! I KNOW *EXACTLY* WHERE WE ARE...WE'RE *LOST!*

HAN, HOW CAN WE BE *LOST?* WE WERE ON A PROGRAMMED COURSE THROUGH HYPERSPACE!

NAVIGATIONAL COMPUTER SEEMS TO HAVE GONE *HAYWIRE,* LUKE...

...BUT DON'T WORRY! I'M *FIXIN'* IT!

CAPTAIN SOLO, THAT'S A DELICATE *MACHINE!* HAVE YOU EVER CONSIDERED *HUMAN* ERROR?

THREEPIO, YOU DON'T *WANT* TO KNOW WHAT I'M CONSIDERIN'!

HAN, CONSIDER FINDING A SAFE PLACE TO *LAND* AND MAKE REPAIRS!

IT'LL BE MUCH EASIER MAKING REPAIRS ON A *PLANET* THAN HERE IN SPACE!

KID, WE'VE HAD A LOTTA *BAD LUCK* ON STRANGE PLANETS. BESIDES...

...I KIND'A *LIKE* SLAMMIN' THIS MALFUNCTIONING SO-AND-SO AROUND.*

THERE'S A *PLANET* IN SIGHT... NO REASON WE CAN'T LAND AND GET TO WORK.

LUKE, YOU *KNOW* THE KIND OF PLACE WE WIND UP IN...THERE'S *ALWAYS* A REASON.*

APPEARS A BIT *TROPICAL*, CAPTAIN SOLO...BUT OTHERWISE IT SEEMS QUITE *LOVELY!*

THE *WORST* KIND.* NOT JUST TROUBLE... *SNEAKY* TROUBLE.*

AFTER ALL OUR TIME IN SPACE, THIS PLANET SEEMS *FINE* TO ME.*

NONE OF OUR WORKING INSTRUMENTS DETECT EVIDENCE OF *IMPERIALS*, MASTER LUKE...

...OR *ANY* SORT OF CIVILIZATION. THE ATMOSPHERE IS SAFE, THE CLIMATE PLEASANT, AND NO TRACE OF DISEASE.

I DON'T *LIKE* IT. IT'S *TOO* NICE.*

Repairs begin on the *MILLENNIUM FALCON*...

WORKING CLOSE TO THAT UNSTABLE SUN WHEN WE HELPED THE ALLIANCE FLEET APPARENTLY *FUSED* SOME ELEMENTS...

...*THAT* AFFECTED YOUR NAVIGATIONAL COMPUTER AND HYPERDRIVE, CAPTAIN SOLO. IN *SPACE*, REPLACING THOSE ELEMENTS MIGHT'VE TAKEN *WEEKS*...

...BUT IN THIS PLANET'S FRIENDLY ATMOSPHERE, ARTOO ESTIMATES--

I CAN'T *STAND* IT! LUKE, YOU GOTTA *DO* SOMETHIN'!

HAN, WHAT'S *WRONG?* THE DROIDS' ESTIMATE OF REPAIRS DOESN'T SOUND BAD. ONCE THE *NAVICOMPUTER'S* FIXED, WE CAN--

SOMETHIN'S GONNA *HAPPEN!*

KID, WE'VE NEVER BEEN *ANYWHERE* WITHOUT RUNNING INTO *SOME* KIND OF BAD NEWS!

BUT... EVERYTHING'S GOING *FINE* HERE!

THAT'S WHAT I *MEAN*, LUKE! THIS PLANET IS *SETTING US UP!* BUT *YOU'RE* GONNA SEE IT DOESN'T SUCCEED!

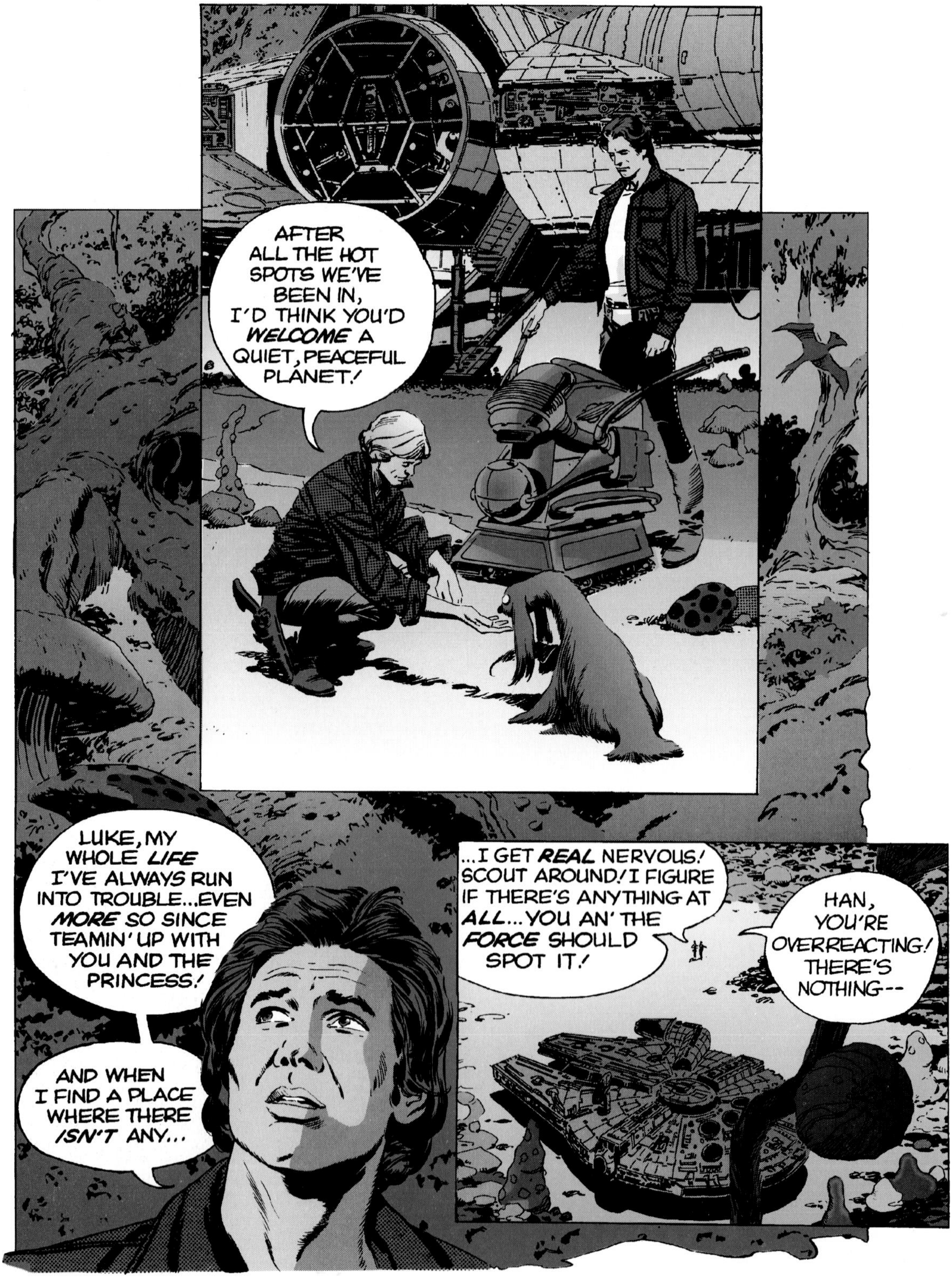

AFTER ALL THE HOT SPOTS WE'VE BEEN IN, I'D THINK YOU'D *WELCOME* A QUIET, PEACEFUL PLANET!
LUKE, MY WHOLE *LIFE* I'VE ALWAYS RUN INTO TROUBLE...EVEN *MORE* SO SINCE TEAMIN' UP WITH YOU AND THE PRINCESS!
AND WHEN I FIND A PLACE WHERE THERE *ISN'T* ANY...
...I GET *REAL* NERVOUS! SCOUT AROUND! I FIGURE IF THERE'S ANYTHING AT *ALL*...YOU AN' THE *FORCE* SHOULD SPOT IT!
HAN, YOU'RE OVERREACTING! THERE'S NOTHING--

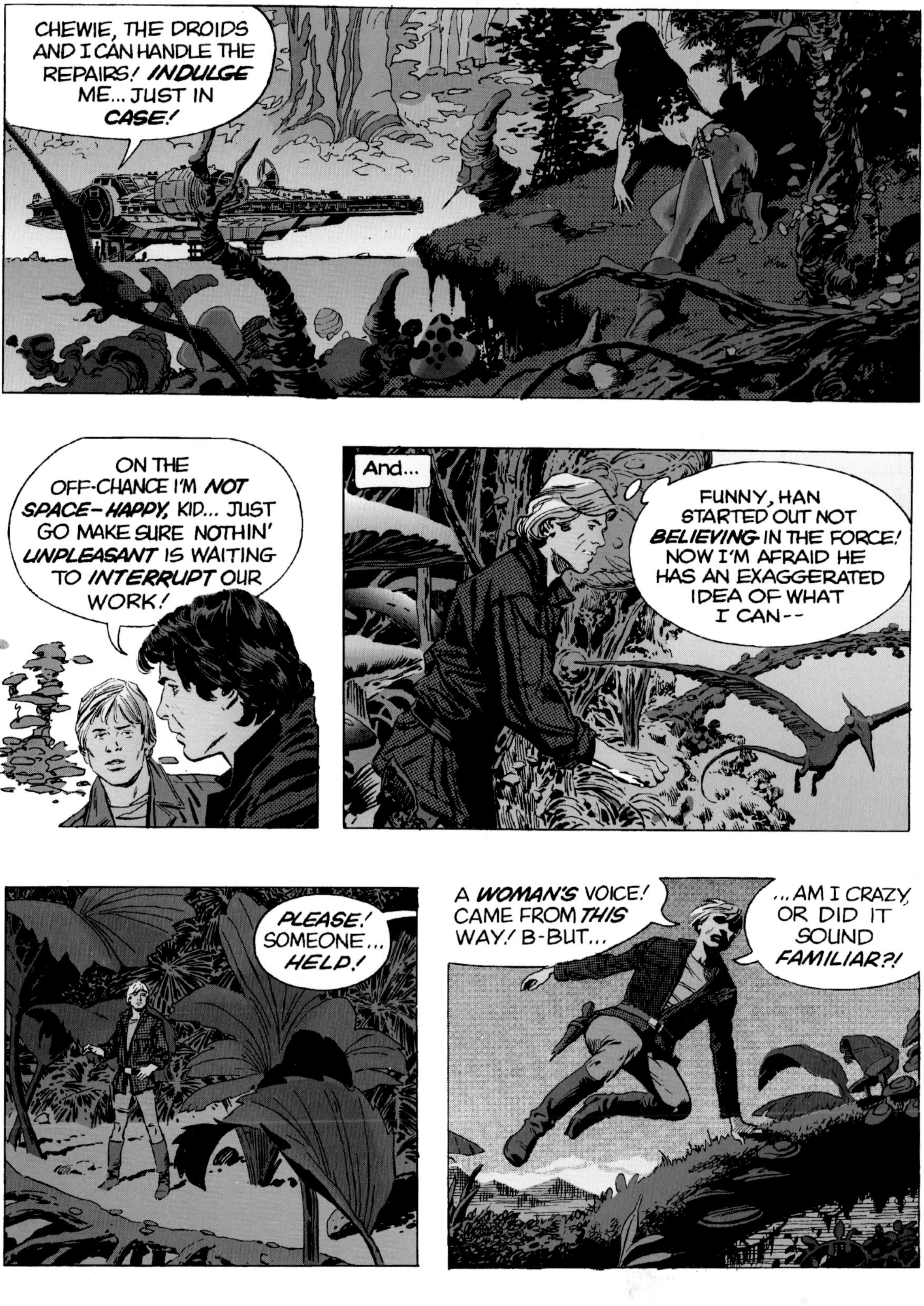
CHEWIE, THE DROIDS AND I CAN HANDLE THE REPAIRS! INDULGE ME... JUST IN CASE!
ON THE OFF-CHANCE I'M NOT SPACE-HAPPY, KID... JUST GO MAKE SURE NOTHIN' UNPLEASANT IS WAITING TO INTERRUPT OUR WORK!
And...
FUNNY, HAN STARTED OUT NOT BELIEVING IN THE FORCE! NOW I'M AFRAID HE HAS AN EXAGGERATED IDEA OF WHAT I CAN--
PLEASE! SOMEONE... HELP!
A WOMAN'S VOICE! CAME FROM THIS WAY! B-BUT...
...AM I CRAZY, OR DID IT SOUND FAMILIAR?!

Luke plunges through the lush tropical foliage, until...

THAT *GIRL!* I *KNOW* HER... *TANITH SHIRE!*

CAN'T RISK A BLASTER SHOT FROM HERE... MIGHT *HIT* HER!

Drawing his lightsaber, Luke charges to the rescue!

TANITH SHIRE SAVED MY *LIFE* WHEN I WAS SPYING ON THE EMPIRE!

DON'T KNOW HOW SHE WOUND UP *HERE*... BUT SHE'S NOT ABOUT TO BECOME *DINNER* FOR SOME WEED WITH DELUSIONS OF GRANDEUR! *NOT IF I CAN HELP IT!*

As Luke slashes to free the girl...

MY *LIGHTSABER!*

T-THING'S FANTASTICALLY *STRONG!* GOT TO REACH... MY BLASTER! *GOT TO!*

But the tentacle-like tendril only pulls Luke's hand *FURTHER* away!

As Luke's hand is pulled *AWAY* from his blaster... the weapon suddenly *LEAPS* across the gap! And...

THANK THE *FORCE!*

IT'S ALL OVER, TANITH. WE'RE *SAFE!* TANITH? *TANITH ?!*

HEY! I JUST SAVED YOU FROM A MAN–EATING PLANT! DON'T RUN AWAY NOW!

TANITH! COME BACK!

THAT'S *TANITH SHIRE*...I'M CERTAIN! I DON'T KNOW *WHY* SHE'D ACT LIKE THIS...

...BUT I'M SURE GOING TO *FIND OUT!* MAYBE SHE'S IN *SHOCK*... NEEDS MEDICAL ATTENTION!

TANITH... *WAIT!* TANITH!

N-NO...!

TANITH, YOU'RE HEADED FOR A *CLIFF!* TANITH!

SHE MUST BE IN *SHOCK* FROM OUR TUSSLE WITH THE CARNIVOROUS PLANT! IF I CAN'T REACH HER IN TIME...

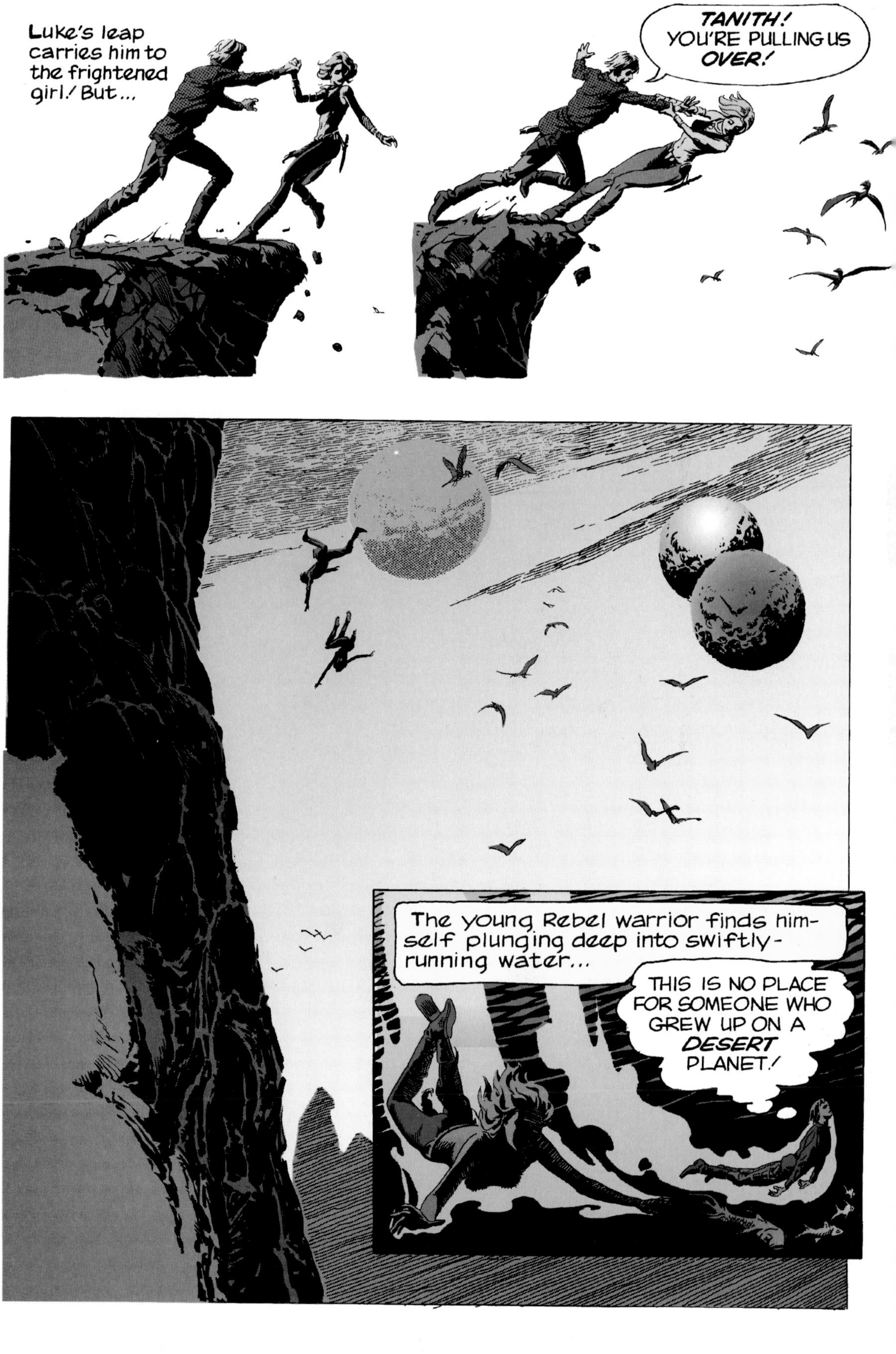
Luke's leap carries him to the frightened girl! But...
TANITH! YOU'RE PULLING US OVER!
The young Rebel warrior finds himself plunging deep into swiftly-running water...
THIS IS NO PLACE FOR SOMEONE WHO GREW UP ON A DESERT PLANET!

Desperately, he fights his way to the surface...

TANITH! TANITH, WHERE **ARE** YOU?!

TANITH! HANG ON! I'VE **GOT** YOU! THE WATER'S NOT SO SWIFT OVER HERE. WE'LL BE OKAY...

TANITH?!

YOU'RE NOT TANITH SHIRE! YOU DON'T LOOK ANYTHING *LIKE* HER!

WHAT'S GOING **ON** AROUND HERE?!

WHO **ARE** YOU?! WHAT MADE ME THINK YOU WERE *TANITH SHIRE*?! YOU DON'T LOOK SIMILAR AT **ALL**!

I AM **S'YBLL** AND I FEAR THE **ATMOSPHERE** OF MY WORLD...

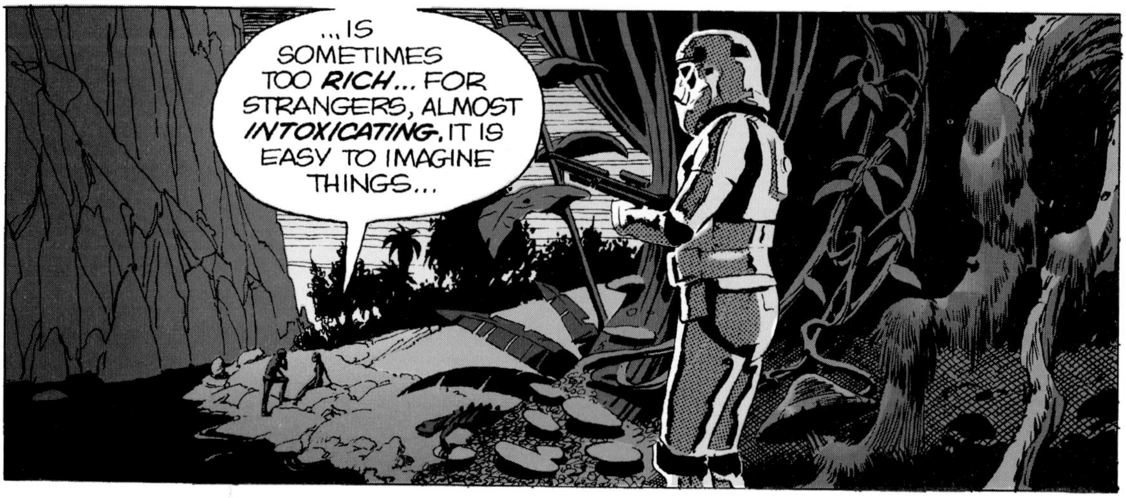
...IS SOMETIMES TOO RICH... FOR STRANGERS, ALMOST INTOXICATING. IT IS EASY TO IMAGINE THINGS...

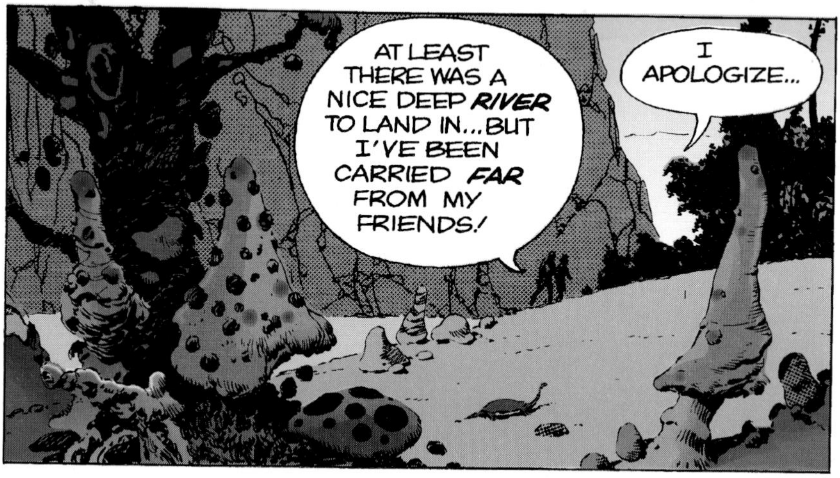
AT LEAST THERE WAS A NICE DEEP RIVER TO LAND IN...BUT I'VE BEEN CARRIED FAR FROM MY FRIENDS!
I APOLOGIZE...

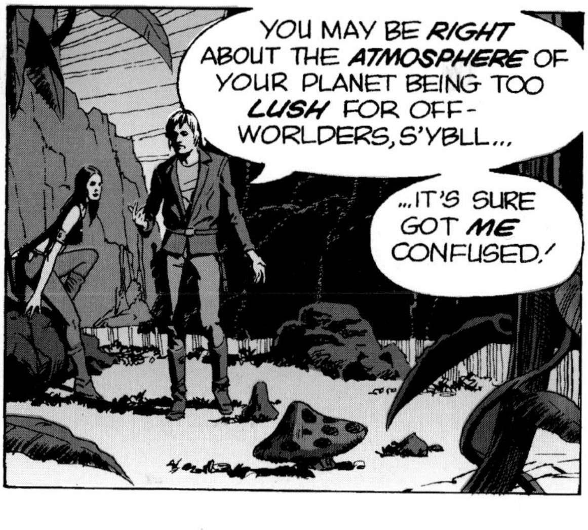
YOU MAY BE RIGHT ABOUT THE ATMOSPHERE OF YOUR PLANET BEING TOO LUSH FOR OFF-WORLDERS, S'YBLL...
...IT'S SURE GOT ME CONFUSED!

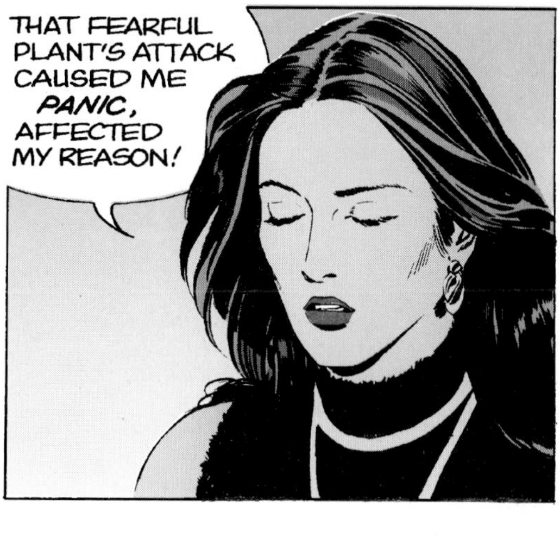
THAT FEARFUL PLANT'S ATTACK CAUSED ME PANIC, AFFECTED MY REASON!

NO MORE THAN *ME*, S'YBLL. HOW COULD I THINK YOU WERE *TANITH SHIRE*... SOMEONE *TOTALLY* DIFFERENT?

I *KNOW* YOU TOLD ME THE ATMOSPHERE OF THIS PLANET IS SO *RICH* IT SOMETIMES GIVES OFF-WORLDERS *ILLUSIONS,* BUT--

IT IS *TRUE!* HOWEVER, YOU WILL NOT BE *LONG* IN ADJUSTING.

GOOD! WONDERING ALL THE TIME IF WHAT I SEE IS *REAL* OR NOT COULD TURN INTO QUITE A...

...PROBLEM!

LOOK *OUT,* S'YBLL! WHATEVER TRICKS YOUR PLANET'S ATMOSPHERE MAY PLAY ON ME...

...I *KNOW* WHEN I'M FACING AN *IMPERIAL STORMTROOPER!* AND--

W-WHAT?!

S'YBLL! THIS IS JUST... AN *EMPTY SUIT* OF STORMTROOPER ARMOR! W-WHY?

I PLACED IT HERE, LUKE... IN HOPE IT MIGHT KEEP *INTRUDERS* AT BAY.

MY *HOME* IS JUST AHEAD.

INTRUDERS? WHAT *KIND* OF INTRUDERS?

MY PLANET APPEARS TO BE A TROPICAL PARADISE, LUKE, BUT THERE *ARE* DANGERS ...WILD BEASTS AND SUCH.

BUT EMPTY *STORMTROOPER ARMOR* FRIGHTENS THEM OFF?

SOMETIMES. PERHAPS IT IS FOOLISH. STILL... IT IS NOT EASY FOR A WOMAN ALONE TO DEFEND HER HOME.

AND *THIS* IS YOUR HOME, S'YBLL?

YOU FIND IT *STRANGE* I USE A *RUIN* AS MY HOME, LUKE?

NO, S'YBLL, *COINCIDENTAL!* UNTIL RECENTLY, REBEL ALLIANCE HEADQUARTERS USED SOMETHING SIMILAR.

WHAT I *DO* FIND STRANGE IS ALL THIS STORMTROOPER *ARMOR*...AND *NO* STORMTROOPERS.! I KEEP WONDERING...WHAT HAPPENED TO THE *MEN* INSIDE?

FIRST, EMPTY SUITS OF STORMTROOPER ARMOR TO GIVE ME A *SCARE*... NOW A SMASHED *IMPERIAL SHUTTLE!* YOU'VE GOT WEIRD TASTE IN *HOME DECORATION*, S'YBLL!

THIS CRAFT LANDED *LONG* BEFORE I SETTLED IN THIS RUIN, LUKE SKYWALKER! *WHATEVER* HAPPENED TO THE SOLDIERS...

...I MERELY PROPPED THEIR *ARMOR* ABOUT TO FRIGHTEN OFF WILD CREATURES!

I WAS ONLY *JOKING*, S'YBLL... DIDN'T MEAN TO INSULT YOUR DEFENSES! BUT I DOUBT THEY'LL STOP ANYTHING THAT COULD DAMAGE A *SHIP* THIS WAY.

THE DAMAGE TO THIS SHUTTLE DIDN'T COME FROM A *CRASH*, S'YBLL. THIS HOLE WAS MADE FROM THE *OUTSIDE*...

...IT'D TAKE SOMETHING PRETTY *TERRIBLE* TO INFLICT THAT!

I TOLD YOU MY PLANET IS NOT *QUITE* THE PARADISE IT APPEARS.

MY PLANET IS *FULL* OF SUCH DANGERS, LUKE! I NEED SOMEONE TO *PROTECT* ME...

...SOMEONE LIKE *YOU*!

S'YBLL...PLEASE. I'LL DO WHAT I *CAN* TO HELP YOU. BUT...I HAVE *OTHER* COMMITMENTS. TO MY FRIENDS...TO THE REBEL ALLIANCE... AND TO--

S'YBLL! WHERE DID YOU *RUN* TO? I DIDN'T MEAN TO *UPSET* YOU, BUT I CAN'T JUST *DESERT* MY FRIENDS HERE AND--

CAPTAIN SOLO...HAVE YOU NOTICED THAT IT'S GROWING *DARK*?

THAT'S 'CAUSE THE *SUN'S* GOIN' DOWN, THREEPIO...HAPPENS A *LOT* THIS TIME OF DAY.

I'M QUITE *AWARE* OF THAT, SIR. I'M ALSO AWARE *MASTER LUKE* HASN'T RETURNED.

YOU'RE THE ONE WHO SAID THE PLANET SEEMED *SAFE*...

"...HE'S PROBABLY JUST DOING A *THOROUGH* JOB OF SCOUTING!'"

" NATURALLY, CAPTAIN SOLO, IF YOU *SAY* NOT TO WORRY ABOUT MASTER LUKE, I *WON'T* WORRY! STILL, IT *DOES* WORRY ME THAT--"

BLAST IT! NOW YOU'VE GOT *ME* WORRIED...

...BUT IF THE KID'S IN TROUBLE, WHY DOESN'T HE *CONTACT* US?

THERE'S **DANGER** IN THE RUINS!

AND I PRAY IT'S **NOT** WHAT IT **APPEARS** TO BE!

PURSUIT! Luke dodges through the jungle ruins... a NIGHTMARE on his heels!

At the *MILLENNIUM FALCON'S* repair site...

THREEPIO, YOU CAN'T REACH LUKE AT *ALL?*

HIS COMLINK IS *OPERATIONAL,* CAPTAIN SOLO, BUT HE'S NOT *RESPONDING!* OH, DEAR...

"...THINGS COULD BE QUITE *DIFFICULT* FOR HIM IF HE'S SOMEHOW *MISPLACED* IT!'"

Luke scrambles for his life!

IF I CAN GET THAT THING TO KEEP COMING AFTER ME... I MIGHT BE ABLE TO USE MY *LIGHTSABER* ON IT!

But...

NO!

Luke's attempt to lure the pursuing monster onto precarious fighting terrain *BACKFIRES*...

...with the crumbling of ancient stone...

...leaving the star warrior from Tatooine helpless... at the **MERCY** of that which approaches!

GIMME THAT COMLINK, THREEPIO! *I'LL* RAISE THE KID!

THERE'S NO *MALFUNCTION*, CAPTAIN SOLO! MASTER LUKE JUST DOESN'T RESPOND! I CAN ONLY CONCLUDE HIS COMLINK IS *LOST*!

WELL, WHY DON'T THEY MAKE 'EM *BIGGER?* SO A GUY ON A DANGEROUS SCOUTING MISSION CAN'T *MISPLACE* 'EM!

CAPTAIN SOLO, IT'S NOW PITCH DARK! THE ODDS AGAINST PICKING UP MASTER LUKE'S *TRAIL* ARE--

DIDN'T THEY PROGRAM YOU WITH ANY *FAVORABLE* STATISTICS, THREEPIO? WE'LL TRY *ANYWAY*!

Meanwhile, a chase through jungle ruins ends disastrously for Luke...

W-WALL I WAS SCALING...COLLAPSED! MONSTER'S RIGHT... *BEHIND* ME! GOT TO GET *UP*...BEFORE IT--

Struggling to regain consciousness after his fall, Luke finds not the looming monster he expects but...

BEN! BEN KENOBI! H-HOW...?

THAT DANGER IS *PAST*, MY BOY. BUT I'M *CONCERNED* FOR YOUR NEW COMPANION, S'YBLL!

BUT WHAT OF YOUR NEW *COMPANION* AND THE DANGERS WHICH MENACE *HER?*

S'YBLL...?

I'M *ALWAYS* WITH YOU, YOUNG LUKE, AND IT SEEMS MY SUDDEN APPEARANCE HAS DRIVEN AWAY THE CREATURE WHICH MENACED YOU.

B-BEN...I'M STILL GROGGY...FROM MY FALL. HOW DID A MONSTER FROM MY *PAST* APPEAR HERE?

WHERE DID IT *GO*?

THERE ARE *MANY* MONSTERS, LUKE, EVEN ON A PLANETARY PARADISE SUCH AS THIS.

THAT IS WHY YOUR NEW FRIEND, S'YBLL, NEEDS YOU, MY BOY. THAT IS WHY YOU *MUST* GO TO HER.

BUT... *HAN* AND THE OTHERS... THE *REBELLION*...

LUKE, THERE ARE *MANY* TO FIGHT THE REBELLION...S'YBLL NEEDS *YOU*.

HAN...THE DROIDS... CHEWBACCA... THEY'RE ALL *WAITING* FOR ME, BEN.

THERE WILL BE TIME FOR THEM LATER, MY BOY. FOR NOW...IT'S *S'YBLL* YOU MUST CONSIDER. GO TO HER.

SHE HID BEFORE THE MONSTER APPEARED...

...WAS IT *HERE*, BEN? YOU WANT ME...TO GO HERE...HELP ME...I FEEL...SO...SO... W-WEAKKKKKK...

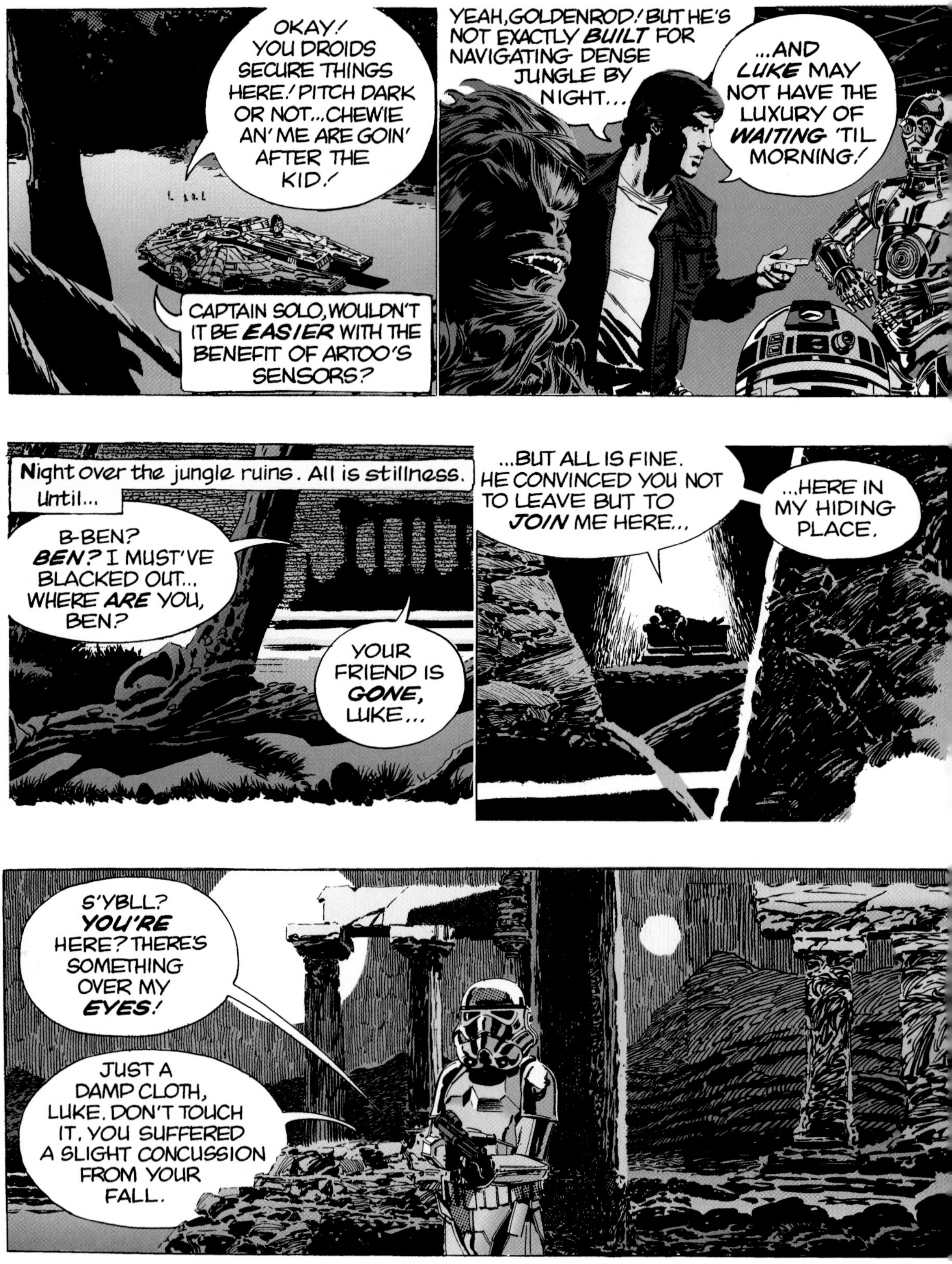
OKAY! YOU DROIDS SECURE THINGS HERE! PITCH DARK OR NOT...CHEWIE AN' ME ARE GOIN' AFTER THE KID!
CAPTAIN SOLO, WOULDN'T IT BE EASIER WITH THE BENEFIT OF ARTOO'S SENSORS?
YEAH, GOLDENROD! BUT HE'S NOT EXACTLY BUILT FOR NAVIGATING DENSE JUNGLE BY NIGHT...
...AND LUKE MAY NOT HAVE THE LUXURY OF WAITING 'TIL MORNING!
Night over the jungle ruins. All is stillness. Until...
B-BEN? BEN? I MUST'VE BLACKED OUT... WHERE ARE YOU, BEN?
YOUR FRIEND IS GONE, LUKE...
...BUT ALL IS FINE. HE CONVINCED YOU NOT TO LEAVE BUT TO JOIN ME HERE...
...HERE IN MY HIDING PLACE.
S'YBLL? YOU'RE HERE? THERE'S SOMETHING OVER MY EYES!
JUST A DAMP CLOTH, LUKE. DON'T TOUCH IT. YOU SUFFERED A SLIGHT CONCUSSION FROM YOUR FALL.

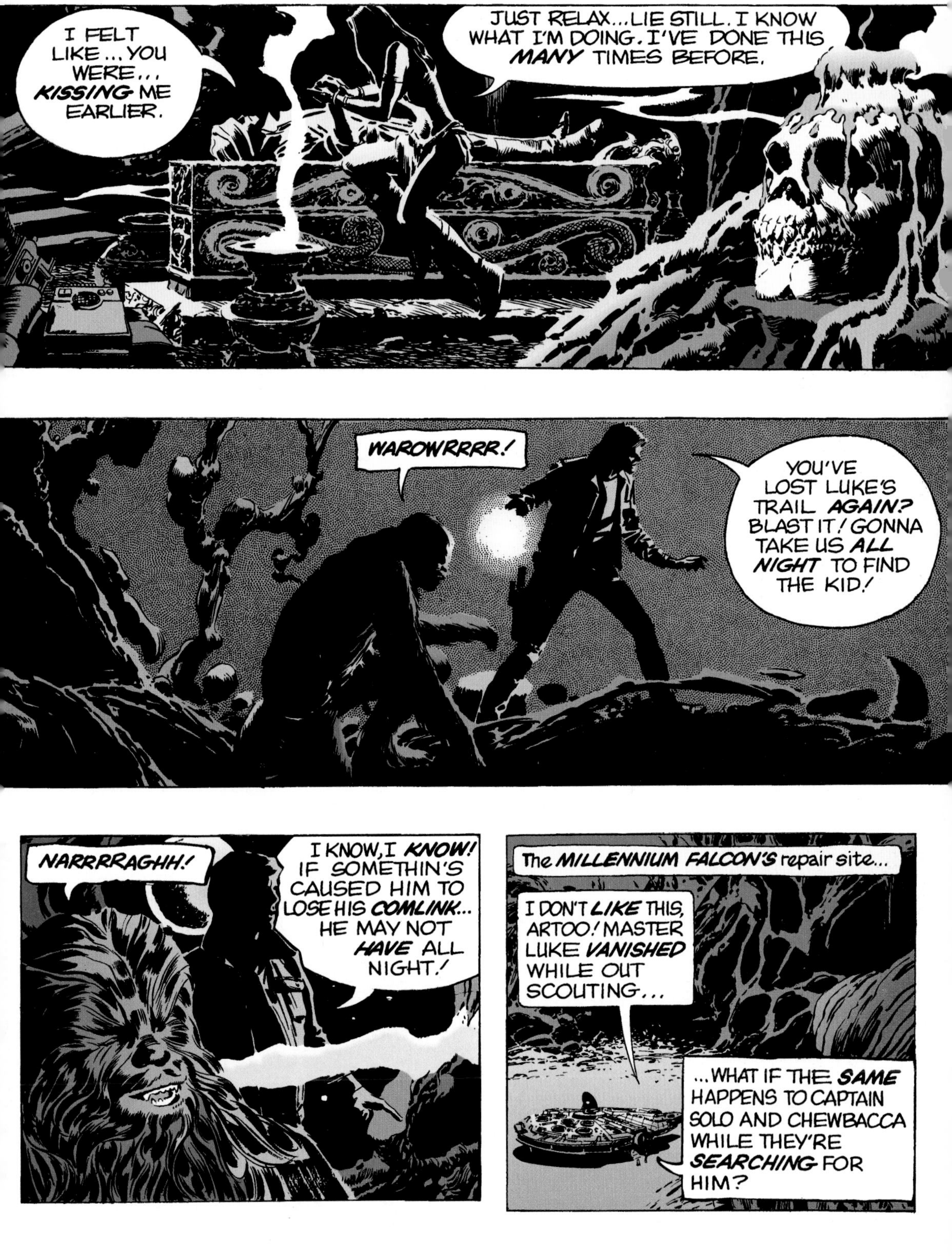
I FELT LIKE... YOU WERE... KISSING ME EARLIER.
JUST RELAX...LIE STILL. I KNOW WHAT I'M DOING. I'VE DONE THIS MANY TIMES BEFORE.
WAROWRRRR!
YOU'VE LOST LUKE'S TRAIL AGAIN? BLAST IT! GONNA TAKE US ALL NIGHT TO FIND THE KID!
NARRRRAGHH!
I KNOW, I KNOW! IF SOMETHIN'S CAUSED HIM TO LOSE HIS COMLINK... HE MAY NOT HAVE ALL NIGHT!
The MILLENNIUM FALCON'S repair site...
I DON'T LIKE THIS, ARTOO! MASTER LUKE VANISHED WHILE OUT SCOUTING...
...WHAT IF THE SAME HAPPENS TO CAPTAIN SOLO AND CHEWBACCA WHILE THEY'RE SEARCHING FOR HIM?

WE'D BE *ABANDONED!*

I CAN'T *STAND* THE NOTION, ARTOO! WE MUST *DO* SOMETHING ...*ANYTHING!*

ARTOO-DETOO! WHERE ARE YOU *GOING?*

VA-DOOTA *BREEEP!*

TO THE *COMMUNICATOR?!* CAPTAIN SOLO LEFT ORDERS NOT TO CALL HIM EXCEPT FOR AN *EMERGENCY!* AND I'M NOT SURE MY *MISGIVINGS* CONSTITUTE--

TRRR-KLIKK VREEP *BLAAT!*

IT'S *MASTER LUKE* YOU WISH TO CONTACT?! BUT... WE *FAILED* AT THAT EARLIER!

S'YBLL? IS IT STILL NIGHT? YOU'VE STAYED HERE WITH ME...SO LONG...

I *LIKE* BEING CLOSE TO YOU, LUKE.

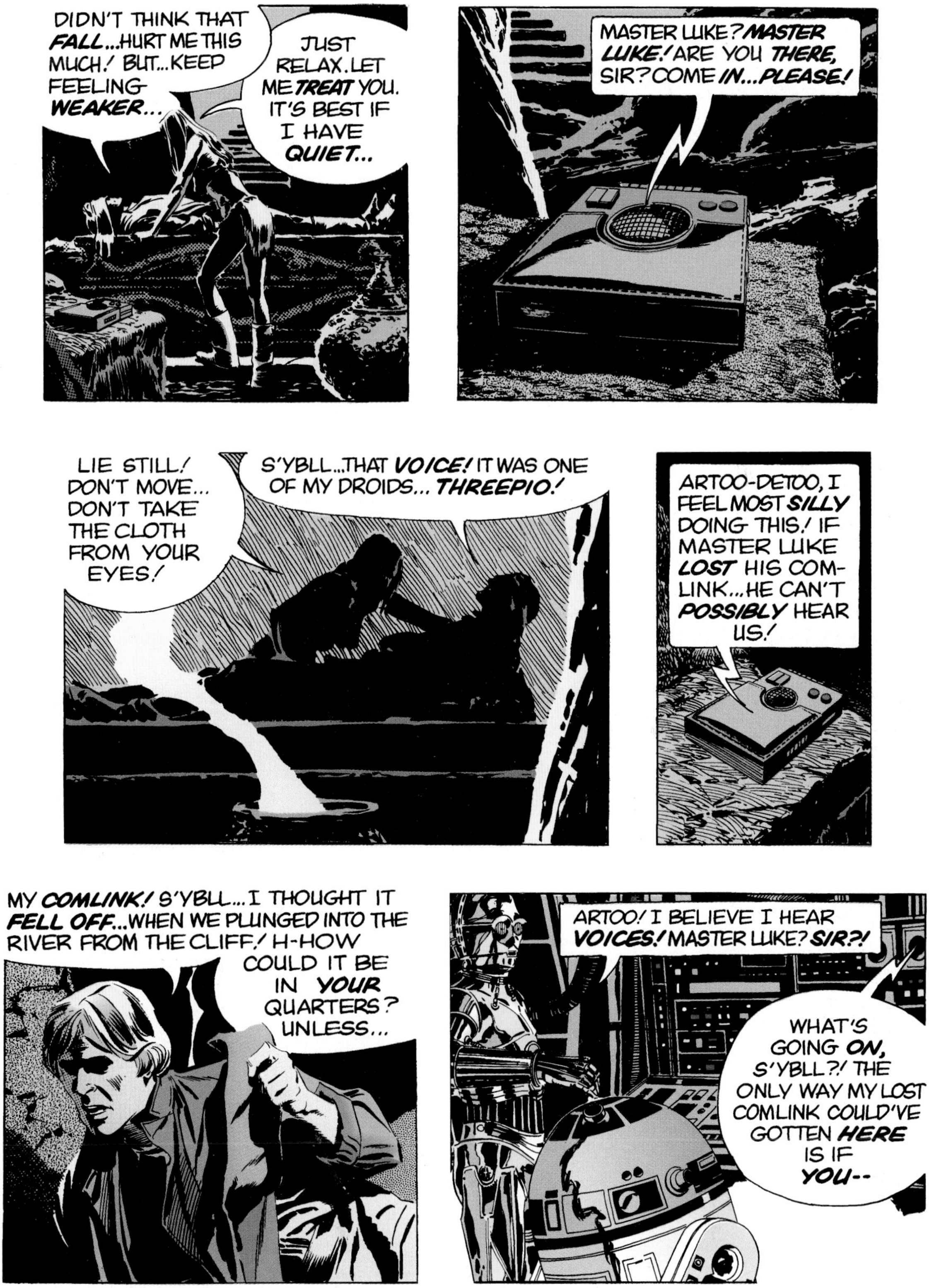
DIDN'T THINK THAT FALL...HURT ME THIS MUCH! BUT...KEEP FEELING WEAKER...
JUST RELAX. LET ME TREAT YOU. IT'S BEST IF I HAVE QUIET...
MASTER LUKE? MASTER LUKE! ARE YOU THERE, SIR? COME IN...PLEASE!
LIE STILL! DON'T MOVE... DON'T TAKE THE CLOTH FROM YOUR EYES!
S'YBLL...THAT VOICE! IT WAS ONE OF MY DROIDS... THREEPIO!
ARTOO-DETOO, I FEEL MOST SILLY DOING THIS! IF MASTER LUKE LOST HIS COM-LINK...HE CAN'T POSSIBLY HEAR US!
MY COMLINK! S'YBLL...I THOUGHT IT FELL OFF...WHEN WE PLUNGED INTO THE RIVER FROM THE CLIFF! H-HOW COULD IT BE IN YOUR QUARTERS? UNLESS...
ARTOO! I BELIEVE I HEAR VOICES! MASTER LUKE? SIR?!
WHAT'S GOING ON, S'YBLL?! THE ONLY WAY MY LOST COMLINK COULD'VE GOTTEN HERE IS IF YOU--

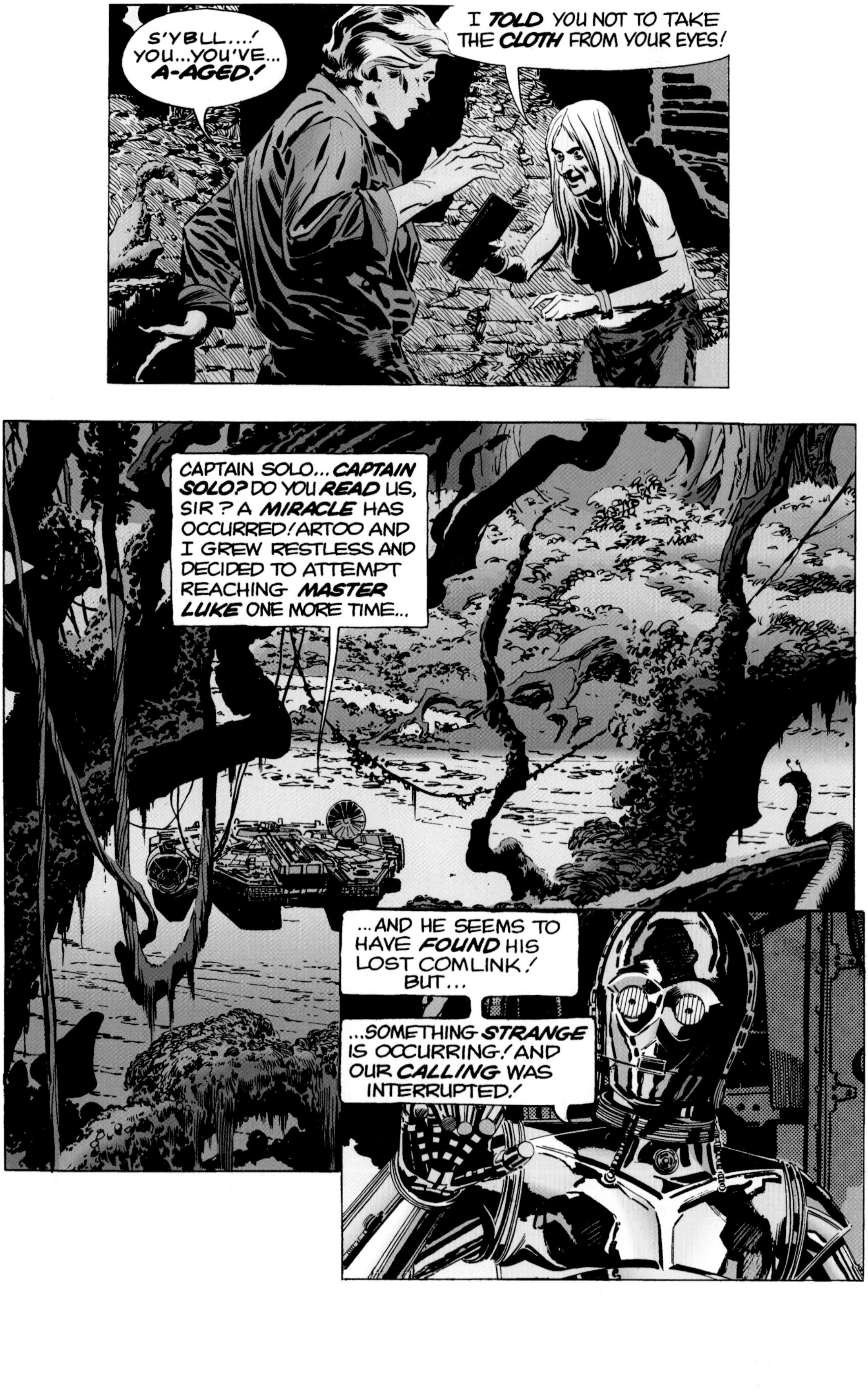

S'YBLL...! YOU...YOU'VE... A-AGED!
I TOLD YOU NOT TO TAKE THE CLOTH FROM YOUR EYES!
CAPTAIN SOLO... CAPTAIN SOLO? DO YOU READ US, SIR? A MIRACLE HAS OCCURRED! ARTOO AND I GREW RESTLESS AND DECIDED TO ATTEMPT REACHING MASTER LUKE ONE MORE TIME...
...AND HE SEEMS TO HAVE FOUND HIS LOST COMLINK! BUT...
...SOMETHING STRANGE IS OCCURRING! AND OUR CALLING WAS INTERRUPTED!

THREEPIO, SLOW DOWN SO CHEWIE AND I CAN *GET* THIS! YOU'VE *CONTACTED* LUKE?

IT'S VERY *CONFUSING*, CAPTAIN SOLO...

...BUT FROM WHAT ARTOO AND I CAN OVERHEAR, SOMEONE APPARENTLY *STOLE* HIS COMLINK! HE'S JUST *DISCOVERED* THIS AND I FEAR THERE'S *DANGER* FROM--

NEVER MIND...

"...JUST GET US A *FIX* ON THE KID'S COMLINK!"

S'YBLL... WHAT'S *H-HAPPENED* TO YOU?!

YOU'RE SEEING ME AS I *AM*, LUKE...UNTIL I'M *FINISHED* WITH YOU!

I'VE *ALWAYS* LOOKED THIS WAY... UNTIL VISITORS LIKE *YOU*-- AND AN IMPERIAL EXPLORATION TEAM BEFORE YOU-- ARRIVE TO *HELP* ME!

AS YOUR *FRIENDS* WILL ARRIVE... FOLLOWING YOUR *COMLINK!*

YOU *STOLE* MY COMLINK, S'YBLL...HID IT HERE...IN YOUR QUARTERS!

YES, LUKE. RIGHT OFF YOUR EQUIPMENT BELT. I WANTED TO *USE* IT LATER...

Y-YOUR **FACE!** SO WITHERED... ANCIENT! HOW...?

...TO LURE YOUR **FRIENDS** TO THESE RUINS **AFTER** I WAS THROUGH WITH **YOU!**

STAND **STILL,** LUKE. YOU'RE TOO WEAK...TOO FAR UNDER MY SPELL...TO ESCAPE **NOW!**

D-DON'T KNOW WHAT YOU'VE **DONE** TO ME... BUT... I WON'T JUST **GIVE UP!**

YES...THERE'S GREAT **POWER** IN YOU. I SENSED THAT...IT'S WHAT **ATTRACTED** ME. BUT IT'S MOSTLY **UNFORMED**...YOU'VE NOT YET **MASTERED** IT...

...AND NOW YOU NEVER **WILL!** I'M GOING TO **DRAIN** YOU OF ALL THAT... AND YOUR **LIFE** AS WELL!

DON'T FIGHT, LUKE...JUST GIVE IN TO MY **EMBRACE!** THE PAIN WON'T LAST LONG...

...I'M A **MIND WITCH!** I WAS ANCIENT WHEN THESE RUINS WERE NEW! I CAN REACH INTO YOUR MEMORIES AND CREATE ILLUSIONS TO ENSNARE AND WEAKEN YOU...

...UNTIL A *PSYCHIC LINK* IS FORGED! THEN I DRAIN THE MENTAL ENERGY FROM YOU... THE VERY LIFE ESSENCE THAT WILL *RENEW* ME... MAKE ME *YOUNG* AGAIN!

THERE'S NO RESISTING, LUKE...YOU'LL SOON BE AN *EMPTY HUSK!* YOUR MENTAL ENERGIES WILL FEED ME... AS DID THOSE OF THE *IMPERIALS* BEFORE YOU!

IT'S *TOO LATE*...EVEN WITH THE *FORCE* RUNNING SO RICHLY WITHIN YOUR BEING! THE HOLD OF THE *MIND WITCH* IS UPON YOU... *GIVE IN!*

S'YBLL...

...NO!

YOU'RE *STRONG!* SO MUCH STRONGER THAN EVEN *I* SUSPECTED!

BUT THE MENTAL LINKS I'VE FORGED INTO YOUR MIND AND MEMORIES ARE STRONGER *STILL!*

YOU CAN'T *FLEE*, LUKE SKYWALKER! YOU'VE *EXHAUSTED* ALL RESERVES... YOU'RE *MINE!*

The droids provide Han and Chewbacca with a fix on Luke's comlink...

DAWN, OL' BUDDY! GOOD THING FOR US...OTHERWISE WE COULDN'T HAVE FOUND A *PATH* DOWN THIS CLIFF!

BUT IT MAY BE *BAD* FOR THE KID! FROM WHAT THREEPIO OVERHEARD, LUKE'S IN *SOME* WEIRD MESS...AN' WE'RE TAKIN' TOO BLASTED *LONG* RUSHIN' TO THE RESCUE!

A tremendous burst of will breaks Luke free of S'ybll's hold, but...

YOUR VERY THOUGHTS... YOUR GREATEST FEARS...ARE MINE TO USE *AGAINST* YOU!

I HAVE YOU *AT LAST*, YOUNG SKYWALKER!

DARTH VADER! Already weakened, Luke RECOILS at the sight!

D-DRIVING ME RIGHT BACK... TO S'YBLL! GOT TO RESIST! IT'S ONLY... ONE OF HER MIND WITCH ILLUSIONS! BUT...

...IT SEEMS SO REAL!

As Luke struggles against the psychic powers of the mind witch, S'ybll...

FIRST WE SCALE DOWN A CLIFF...NOW A RIVER TO CROSS!

CHEWIE, THIS HAS TO BE THE GALAXY'S SLOWEST RESCUE! BY THE TIME WE FINISH FIGHTIN' THAT CURRENT... THE KID MAY BE FINISHED TOO!

WAURRRGH!

HEY! WHATTA YOU DOIN'?! HAVE YOU GONE NUTS, YA BIG FURBALL?!

Seizing his protesting partner, Chewbacca scales a nearby tree! And...

YEEEOOWWW! CHEWIE, YOU FOUND A FAST WAY TO CROSS THE *RIVER*, BUT WHAT IF THE *VINE*...

...CAN'T *HOLD* OUR WEIGHT?!

In the jungle ruins...

C-CAN'T LET AN ILLUSION CREATED FROM MY OWN *FEARS* DRIVE ME BACK INTO S'YBLL'S CLUTCHES! INSTEAD OF *RESISTING* IT...

I'VE GOT TO *STOP* AND BE *CALM!*

HIS LIGHTSABER IS PASSING *THROUGH* ME... *HARMLESSLY!*

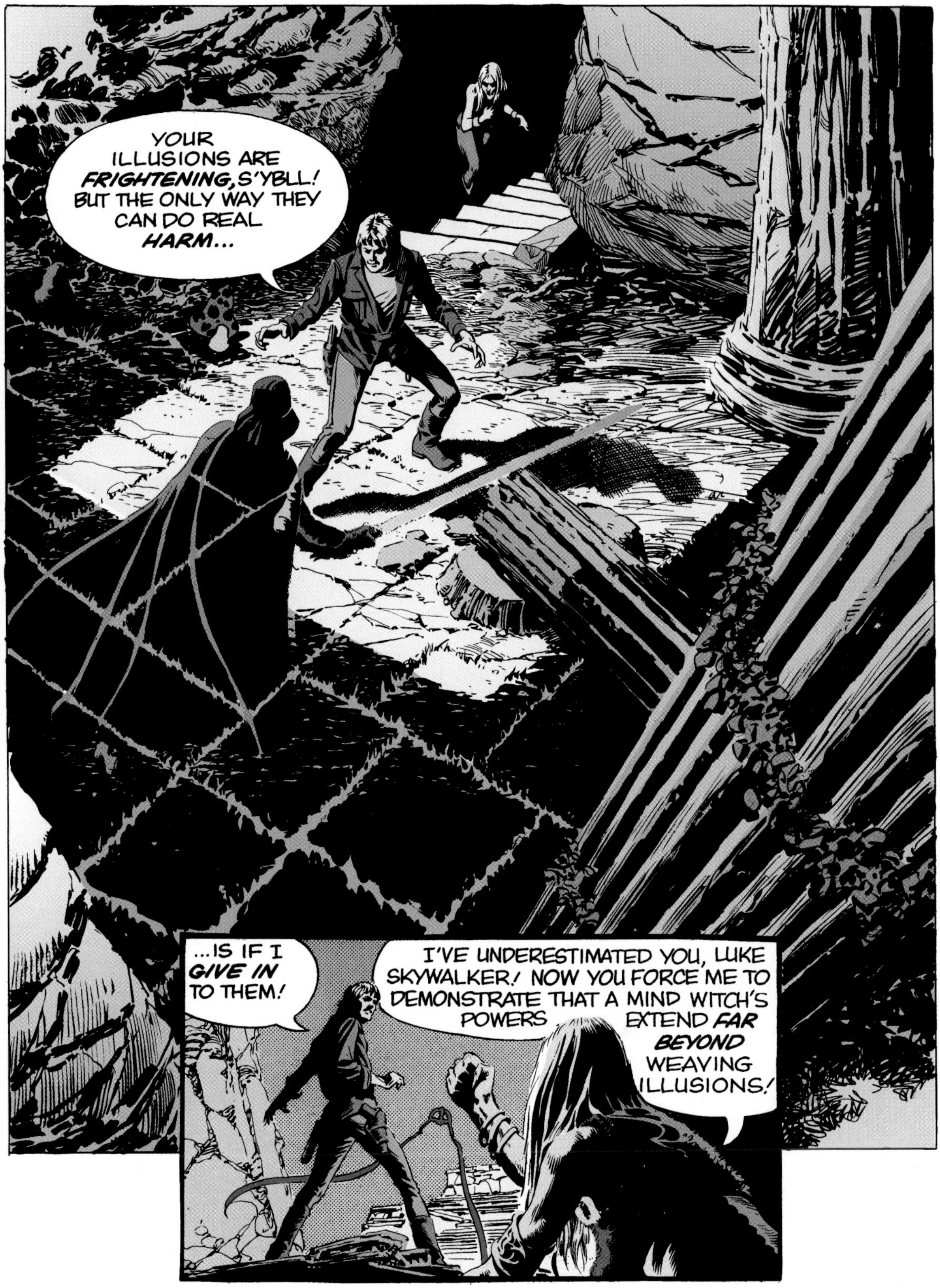
YOUR ILLUSIONS ARE FRIGHTENING, S'YBLL! BUT THE ONLY WAY THEY CAN DO REAL HARM...
...IS IF I GIVE IN TO THEM!
I'VE UNDERESTIMATED YOU, LUKE SKYWALKER! NOW YOU FORCE ME TO DEMONSTRATE THAT A MIND WITCH'S POWERS EXTEND FAR BEYOND WEAVING ILLUSIONS!

I CAN WIELD *PHYSICAL OBJECTS!* I HATE TO CRUSH A SOURCE OF *MENTAL ENERGIES* WHICH CAN FEED AND *RENEW* ME,...

...BUT YOUR *FRIENDS* SHOULD ARRIVE SOON TO *REPLACE* YOU...

...AND THEY'LL BE EVEN *EASIER* TO CONTEND WITH!

And...

TOO BAD THE *VINE BROKE!*

AT LEAST IT GOT US *BEYOND* THE WORST CURRENTS... AN' *CLOSER* TO SAVIN' LUKE!

LUKE! *LUKE?!* IT'S HAN AND CHEWIE! YOU *AROUND,* KID? WHAT WAS THAT *CRASH* WE HEARD?!

THIS WAY!

HURRY! *PLEASE!* YOUR FRIEND'S BEEN *HURT!*

NOT AS FATALLY AS YOU *THINK,* S'YBLL!

YOU'VE WEAKENED ME, S'YBLL...BUT NOT SO MUCH I COULDN'T DODGE ONE FALLING ROCK!

YOU DARE *TAUNT* ME?! PERHAPS YOU NEED A *FINAL* DEMONSTRATION, LUKE SKYWALKER...

...OF JUST *HOW FAR* A MIND WITCH'S ABILITY TO MOVE PHYSICAL OBJECTS CAN *GO!*

And the loose stones of the ancient jungle ruin *seem* to come alive!

A STORM OF STONE! The enraged mind witch turns the entire ruins into a weapon against Luke!

LIKE A... *METEOR SHOWER!* CAN'T HOLD ON LONG...IF I'VE GUESSED *INCORRECTLY!*

And...

CHEWIE! WHAT'S GOIN' *ON?!* FIRST SOMEBODY *CALLS* US...THEN THE WHOLE PLACE STARTS *FLYIN' APART!* NOW...

...IT'S SUDDENLY *QUIET...*AS A *TOMB!*

LUKE! CHEWIE, THE DROIDS AND I HAVE BEEN BLASTED *WORRIED!* WHAT *HAPPENED* HERE, KID?

I MADE SOMEONE VERY *ANGRY,* HAN...

A *MIND WITCH!* S'YBLL MEANT TO *RENEW* HERSELF BY DRAINING ALL OF OUR MENTAL ENERGIES!

THIS PLACE LOOKED LIKE IT WAS *COMIN' APART,* LUKE!

IT WAS LIKE A *METEOR STORM* FOR A WHILE...

...SHE *EXHAUSTED* THE LAST OF HER *OWN* ENERGIES TRYING TO KILL ME! AND WITHOUT ANYTHING TO *SUSTAIN* HER... SHE COLLAPSED AS SHE SHOULD HAVE *AGES* AGO!

AND YOU GOADED HER INTO *DOIN'* IT?

SHE MEANT TO KILL ME AND *RENEW* HERSELF BY DRAINING *YOU TWO* OF YOUR MENTAL ENERGIES! I GAMBLED THAT IF SHE GOT *ENRAGED* ENOUGH...

...THE EFFORT WOULD EXHAUST HER *OWN* ENERGIES INSTEAD! AND *WITHOUT* THEM, THE AGES SHE'D LIVED TOOK THEIR *TOLL!*

INSTEAD 'A THE TOLL SHE WAS GONNA TAKE OF *US!* KID... TIME WE *LEFT* THIS PARADISE!

Meanwhile, concern mounts in the newly established Rebel base on Hoth.

STILL **NOTHING** ON THE **MILLENNIUM FALCON?** HOW COULD IT JUST **VANISH?!**

PRINCESS LEIA! WE'VE JUST **HEARD** FROM CAPTAIN SOLO AND COMMANDER SKYWALKER! THEY'RE ON THEIR WAY! BUT...THERE'S A SERIOUS **COMPLICATION!**

And as the **MILLENNIUM FALCON** finally makes its way to the **HOTH SYSTEM!**

WE MADE IT, LUKE... DESPITE BEING FORCED TO STOP FOR REPAIRS!

EVERYBODY AT THE NEW BASE PROBABLY GAVE US UP FOR LOST! I CAN IMAGINE THE **WARM WELCOME** WE'RE GONNA GET, KID...

"...ESPECIALLY FROM HER ROYALNESS!"

HAN SOLO! YOU BANTHA-BRAINED EXCUSE FOR A SMUGGLER! YOU'VE JEOPARDIZED **EVERYTHING!**

DO YOU **KNOW** WHAT YOU'VE DONE COMING BACK THIS WAY, HAN?

I **THOUGHT** I WAS REJOININ' SOMEBODY WHO **MIGHT** BE GLAD TO SEE ME...

...OR AT LEAST BE PLEASED TO HAVE AN IMPORTANT REBEL ALLIANCE *HERO* LIKE COMMANDER SKYWALKER HERE RETURNED!

LISTEN, YOU TWO...

...MAYBE IF YOU'D STOP *FIGHTING* FOR A SECOND, WE COULD GET IN FROM THE COLD AND FIND OUT WHAT THE *REAL* PROBLEM IS!

HEY! GENERAL RIEEKAN'S CREW DID *SOME* JOB WHILE THE REST OF US WERE ESCAPING THE *OLD* BASE!

IT'S A *NEW BEGINNING* FOR THE REBEL ALLIANCE, HAN...

...BUT BECAUSE OF THE *TIMING* OF YOUR RETURN, IT COULD VERY WELL BE THE *END!*

KEEPING THE LOCATION OF THIS BASE *SECRET* IS VITAL TO THE *SURVIVAL* OF THE REBEL ALLIANCE, HAN!

ALL WE DID WAS *RETURN...*

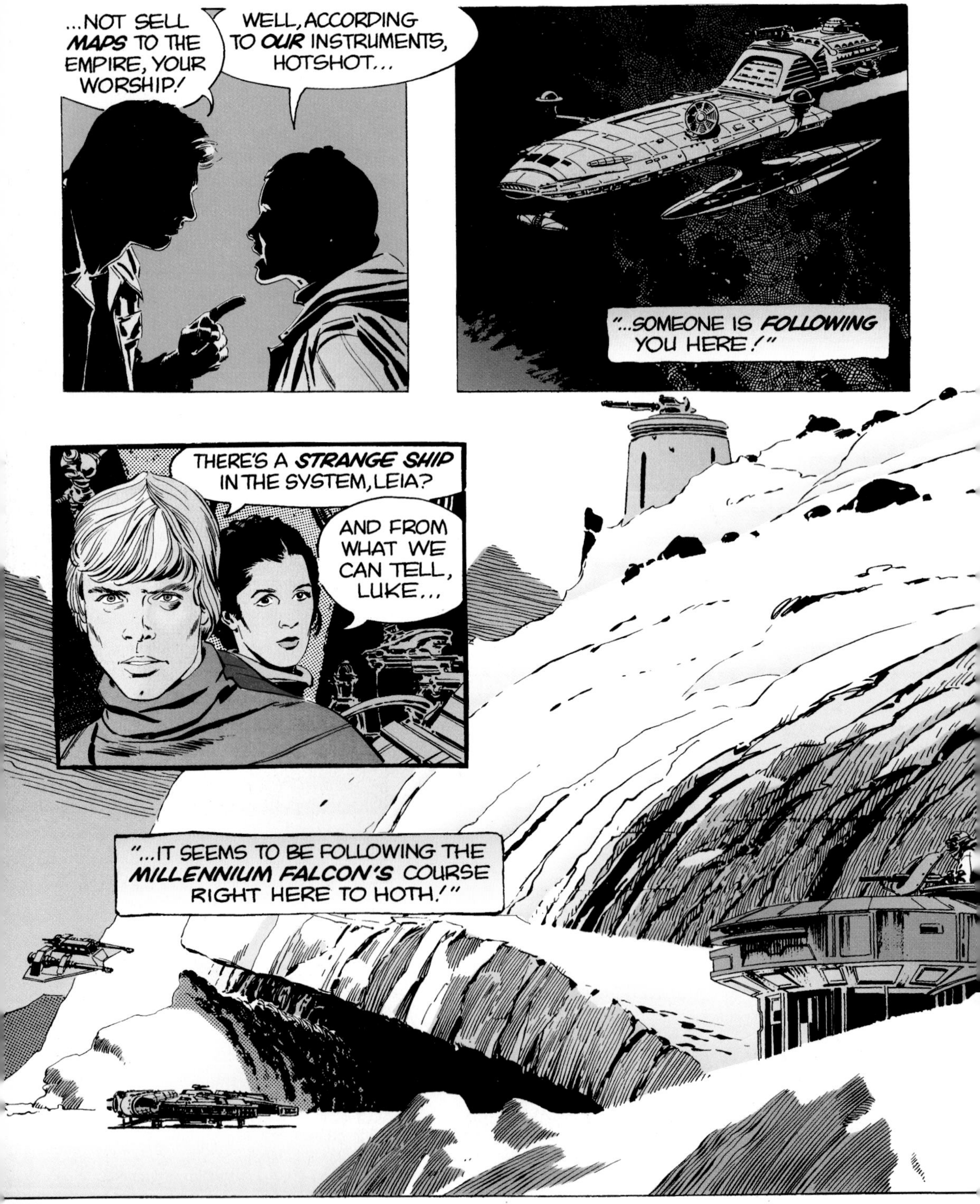
...NOT SELL MAPS TO THE EMPIRE, YOUR WORSHIP!
WELL, ACCORDING TO OUR INSTRUMENTS, HOTSHOT...
"...SOMEONE IS FOLLOWING YOU HERE!"
THERE'S A STRANGE SHIP IN THE SYSTEM, LEIA?
AND FROM WHAT WE CAN TELL, LUKE...
"...IT SEEMS TO BE FOLLOWING THE MILLENNIUM FALCON'S COURSE RIGHT HERE TO HOTH!"

I CAN'T *BELIEVE* ANYONE FOLLOWED THE *FALCON* HERE!

SHE SPORTS THE BEST *DETECTION SYSTEM* ANY SMUGGLIN' SHIP EVER HAD!

EXCUSE ME, CAPTAIN, MAY I REMIND YOU THAT TO COMPLETE THE REPAIRS NECESSARY FOR OUR RETURN, YOU JURY-RIGGED A POWER *BYPASS* OF THE DETECTION SYSTEM?

"IT DOESN'T MATTER NOW. THE IMPORTANT THING IS HOW WE CAN *UNDO* THE DAMAGE BEFORE THAT SHIP APPROACHING *DISCOVERS* THIS BASE!"

LOOK, YOUR ROYALNESS, WHAT'S THE *FUSS* ABOUT? IF THAT SHIP *REALLY* WORRIES YOU...

...SEND UP SOME *X-WINGS* AND BLOW IT *AWAY!*

EXACTLY THE SORT OF MUSH-MINDED SOLUTION I'D *EXPECT* OF THE MAN WHO *CREATED* THIS PROBLEM.'

I DIDN'T CREATE ANY *PROBLEM*, LEIA... I JUST DID WHAT I *HAD* TO DO TO *REJOIN* YOUR PRECIOUS REBELLION!

LIKE SACRIFICING YOUR SHIP'S *DETECTION SYSTEM*...

...TO GET POWER FOR THAT FLYING JUNK HEAP'S *HYPERDRIVE!*

OH, DEAR! PERHAPS I SHOULDN'T HAVE REMINDED CAPTAIN *SOLO* OF THAT WITHIN THE PRINCESS'S *HEARING!*

THOSE *REPAIRS* ENABLED THAT *STRANGE SHIP* TO FOLLOW YOU, HOTSHOT! OUR NEW BEGINNING HERE ON HOTH MAY BE *OVER*... UNLESS *YOU* DO SOMETHING!

LISTEN, LADY, THAT STRANGE SHIP IS *EVERYBODY'S* PROBLEM! WHY DO *I* HAVE TO BE THE ONE WHO *DOES* SOMETHING ABOUT IT?

BECAUSE IF IT EVEN *GLIMPSES* A REBEL SHIP, OUR PRESENCE HERE COULD BE REPORTED TO THE *EMPIRE* BEFORE WE JAM COMMUNICATIONS!

"SO HOP BACK IN YOUR FLYING ANTIQUE AND LEAD THE INTRUDER *AWAY*, CAPTAIN... BE IT FRIEND, FOE, OR SOMETHING WE CAN'T EVEN *IMAGINE!*"

LEMME TELL YOU, CHEWIE... THIS IS THE LAST REBELLION, AND *ESPECIALLY* THE LAST *PRINCESS,* I EVER GET INVOLVED WITH!

HAN... *WAIT!* I'M COMING ALONG!

SOMETIMES I THINK IF YOU AND LEIA DIDN'T *FIGHT*...YOU WOULDN'T HAVE ANYTHING TO *TALK* ABOUT!

KID, YOU HAVEN'T *SEEN* A FIGHT...

...UNTIL I COME BACK FROM *VAPORIZING* THAT INTRUDER AND *REALLY* QUARREL WITH HER ROYALNESS!

THAT'S *TWO* THINGS I CAME ALONG TO *PREVENT!*

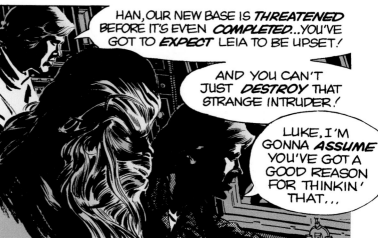

HAN, OUR NEW BASE IS *THREATENED* BEFORE IT'S EVEN *COMPLETED*...YOU'VE GOT TO *EXPECT* LEIA TO BE UPSET!

AND YOU CAN'T JUST *DESTROY* THAT STRANGE INTRUDER!

LUKE, I'M GONNA *ASSUME* YOU'VE GOT A GOOD REASON FOR THINKIN' THAT...

...BUT I KINDA *WONDER* IF THE OTHER SHIP WILL FEEL SO REASONABLE ABOUT *US!*

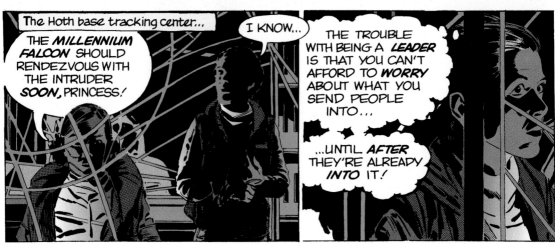

The Hoth base tracking center...

THE *MILLENNIUM FALCON* SHOULD RENDEZVOUS WITH THE INTRUDER *SOON,* PRINCESS!

I KNOW...

THE TROUBLE WITH BEING A *LEADER* IS THAT YOU CAN'T AFFORD TO *WORRY* ABOUT WHAT YOU SEND PEOPLE INTO...

...UNTIL *AFTER* THEY'RE ALREADY *INTO* IT!

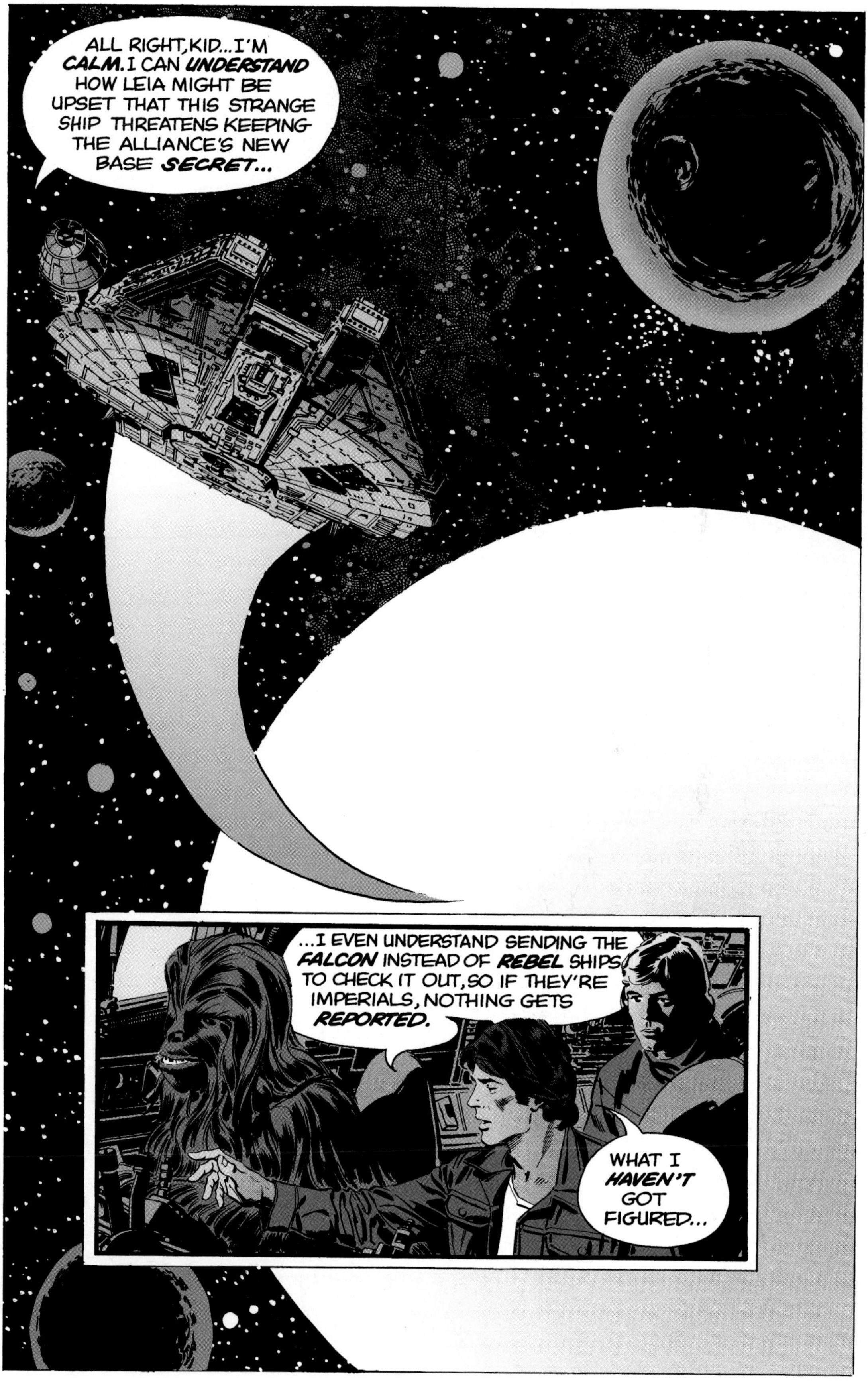
ALL RIGHT, KID...I'M CALM. I CAN UNDERSTAND HOW LEIA MIGHT BE UPSET THAT THIS STRANGE SHIP THREATENS KEEPING THE ALLIANCE'S NEW BASE SECRET...
...I EVEN UNDERSTAND SENDING THE FALCON INSTEAD OF REBEL SHIPS TO CHECK IT OUT, SO IF THEY'RE IMPERIALS, NOTHING GETS REPORTED.
WHAT I HAVEN'T GOT FIGURED...

...IS WHY YOU'RE SO *AGAINST* US COMIN' IN *BLASTING!*

BESIDES THE UNLIKELY CHANCE THEY'RE *FRIENDLY,* HAN, WHAT WOULD AROUSE THE EMPIRE'S INTEREST *MORE...*

...THAN HAVING A SPYCRAFT SUDDENLY *DISAPPEAR?*

I WAS *AFRAID* YOU HAD A GOOD ANSWER... *NOW* WHAT DO WE DO?!

As the *MILLENNIUM FALCON* approaches the ship that has followed it toward Hoth...

IF THEY'RE IMPERIAL SPIES, THAT WOULD ALERT THE EMPIRE THAT *SOMETHING'S* WRONG IN THIS SYSTEM...

...ARE YOU *SURE* WE CAN'T BLOW 'EM AWAY?

WELL, WE'VE *RULED OUT* THAT THEY'RE *FRIENDLY,* LUKE...

...AND START AN INVESTIGATION THAT WOULD REVEAL OUR *BASE!* WE'VE GOT TO BE *CLEVER* ABOUT THIS, HAN... WE'VE GOT TO... *LET THEM CAPTURE US!*

WHAT?!

LUKE, YOU'RE A *FRIEND*...BUT YOU'RE TRYING MY *PATIENCE!* I'M A PIRATE, A *SMUGGLER*...TO WILLINGLY *SURRENDER* MY SHIP...

...*VIOLATES* EVERYTHING I *STAND* FOR!

VARARRWWK!

THAT WAS *DIFFERENT*, CHEWIE...THERE WAS *MONEY* INVOLVED!

HAN, THE ENTIRE *REBELLION'S* INVOLVED IF THE LOCATION OF OUR *BASE* IS REVEALED! YOU'VE *GOT* TO DO IT...

...*PLEASE!*

MAYBE WE CAN'T *FIGHT* THESE GUYS, LUKE...BUT I'D RATHER GIVE 'EM A GOOD *CHASE* THAN SURRENDER!

HAN, EVEN IF YOU *LOSE* THEM...

...WE'VE AROUSED THEIR *CURIOSITY!* THE *BEST* WAY TO PROTECT OUR BASE ON HOTH... IS TO CONVINCE THEM WE'VE SOME *OTHER* REASON FOR BEING HERE!

AND WE'VE GOT TO *GIVE UP* TO DO THAT? OKAY, KID... I HOPE THEY'LL TAKE US IN *ONE* PIECE!

HEY! THIS IS THE *MILLENNIUM FALCON!* DON'T KNOW WHY YOU GUYS ARE BLASTIN' A PEACEFUL *FREIGHTER,* BUT SINCE WE'RE IN NO SHAPE TO *FIGHT,* HOW 'BOUT LETTIN' US *TALK?*

The only response to Han's communication is...

A *TRACTOR BEAM!* LUKE, IF YOU'RE *WRONG* ABOUT WHAT WE'RE DOIN'... IT'S *TOO LATE!*

Elsewhere on the unidentified craft...

WE *HAVE* THEM, SIR. FURTHER ORDERS?

WHY, CONTACT *JABBA THE HUTT,* OF COURSE!

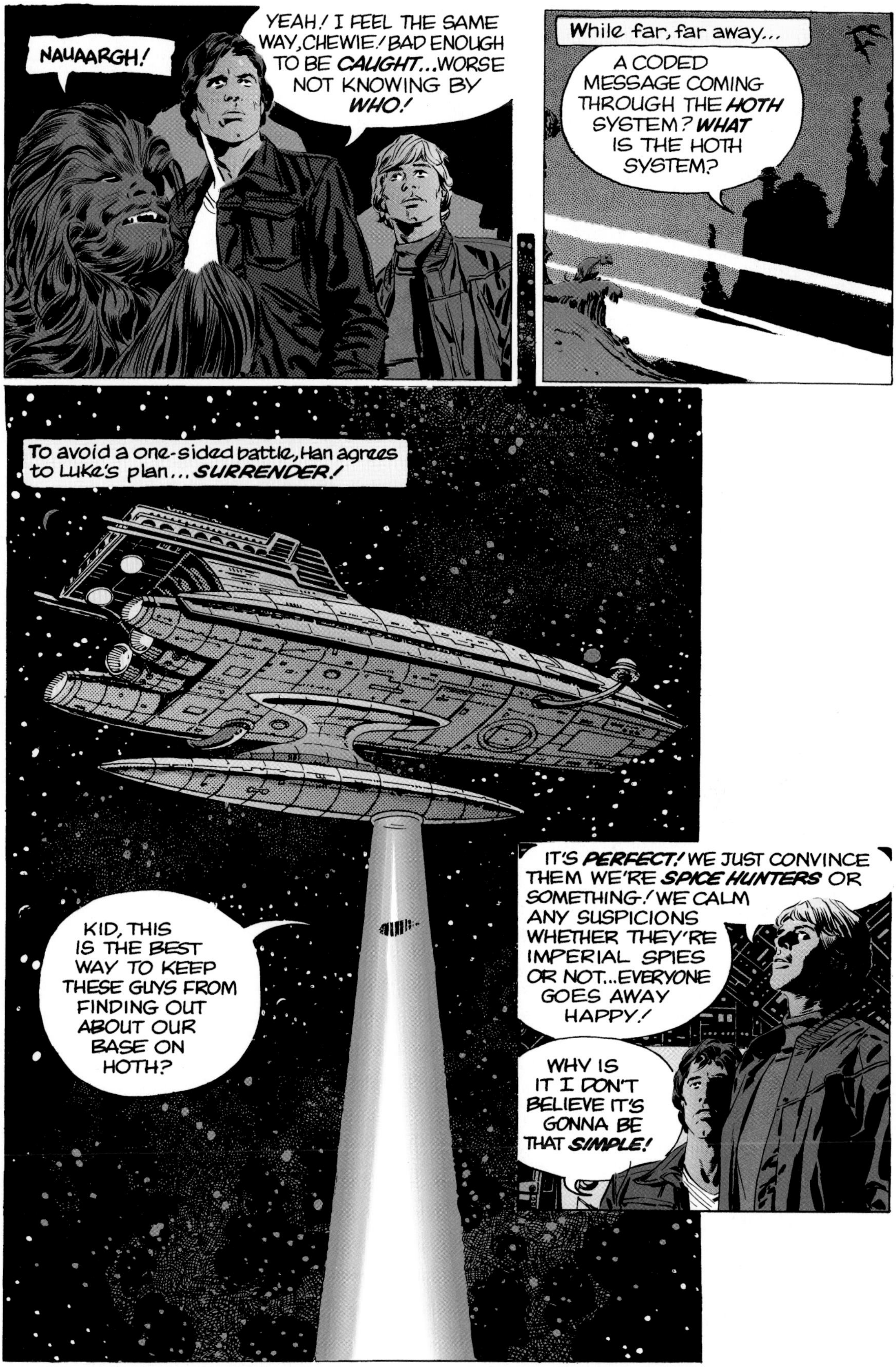
NAUAARGH!
YEAH! I FEEL THE SAME WAY, CHEWIE! BAD ENOUGH TO BE CAUGHT... WORSE NOT KNOWING BY WHO!
While far, far away...
A CODED MESSAGE COMING THROUGH THE HOTH SYSTEM? WHAT IS THE HOTH SYSTEM?
To avoid a one-sided battle, Han agrees to Luke's plan... SURRENDER!
KID, THIS IS THE BEST WAY TO KEEP THESE GUYS FROM FINDING OUT ABOUT OUR BASE ON HOTH?
IT'S PERFECT! WE JUST CONVINCE THEM WE'RE SPICE HUNTERS OR SOMETHING! WE CALM ANY SUSPICIONS WHETHER THEY'RE IMPERIAL SPIES OR NOT...EVERYONE GOES AWAY HAPPY!
WHY IS IT I DON'T BELIEVE IT'S GONNA BE THAT SIMPLE!

As the *MILLENNIUM FALCON* is captured by the unidentified craft, a *MESSAGE* is sent across the galaxy...

...TO JABBA THE HUTT!

MASTER! A *CODED MESSAGE!* SENT FAR ACROSS THE GALAXY TO TATOOINE! SOMEWHERE CALLED THE *HOTH SYSTEM!*

IT CONCERNS YOUR *REWARD* FOR *HAN SOLO!*

SOMEONE IN THE *HOTH* SYSTEM HAS CAPTURED *SOLO?!* WHERE *IS* THIS SYSTEM?

ON NO STANDARD CHARTS, MIGHTY JABBA...

...AND THE MESSAGE WAS *CODED* SO IT COULD NOT BE TRACED TO ITS POINT OF ORIGIN! BUT THE SENDER DOES NOT *SAY* HE HAS SOLO...

...HE MERELY WISHES TO KNOW *HOW MUCH* YOU WILL PAY *IF* HE ACQUIRES THE CAPTAIN!

GAMES! JABBA DOES NOT *PLAY* GAMES!

THE CHANNEL IS STILL *OPEN,* MAGNIFICENT ONE! I WILL TELL THIS STRANGER HE *OFFENDS* YOU AND--

NO! GIVE HIM THE *REWARD* INFORMATION... BUT QUESTION OUR MYSTERIOUS "FRIEND" ABOUT HOW *CLOSE* HE IS TO DELIVERING HAN SOLO!

IF HIS NEGOTIATIONS GROW *TOO* COMPLICATED... WE HAVE *ALTERNATIVES!*

TRACTOR BEAM OFF! *MILLENNIUM FALCON* SECURE IN THE HOLD!

LET THEM SWEAT A BIT WHILE I AWAIT MY *ANSWER* FROM--

THE REPLY FROM *JABBA THE HUTT,* SIR!

AH! AS I HOPED... HE'S RECENTLY *RAISED* THE REWARD FOR HAN SOLO!

NO LIGHTS OUT IN THE HOLD, LUKE! WHO *ARE* THEY? WHAT ARE THEY *WAITING* FOR?

MAYBE THEY'RE JUST *CAUTIOUS,* HAN... MAYBE.

IF THEY DON'T *DO* SOMETHIN' SOON, I'M GONNA --

MILLENNIUM FALCON! LOWER YOUR RAMP! COME OUT IMMEDIATELY! YOU WON'T *LIKE* IT IF WE HAVE TO COME *IN!*

LISTEN! WE'RE A *PEACEFUL FREIGHTER,* JUST IN THIS SYSTEM TO... TO...

WE'RE *SPICE HUNTERS!*

STRANGE! THE *MILLENNIUM FALCON* I REMEMBER WAS USED FOR SMUGGLING, PIRACY, AND OCCASIONAL MISSIONS FOR THE *REBELLION!* IS *HAN SOLO* NO LONGER THE OWNER?

CAN'T *SEE* WHO WE'RE TALKIN' TO OUT IN THE HOLD... BUT THAT *VOICE!* I *KNOW* THAT VOICE!

AND I KNOW *YOUR* VOICE, HAN SOLO! LET'S NOT WASTE *TIME* CONVERSING BY COMLINK...

...COME OUT *NOW!*

A communications exchange arouses Jabba the Hutt's curiosity...and wrath!

WHO ARE WE **DEALING** WITH, BIB FORTUNA?! DOES HE **HAVE** HAN SOLO...OR **NOT?!**

HE REMAINED **VAGUE,** O GREAT ONE, BUT EXPRESSED PLEASURE THAT YOU'VE RECENTLY **RAISED** THE REWARD.

I REWARD **RESULTS**...NOT COY **HINTS!** HOWEVER OBSCURE THIS HOTH SYSTEM MAY BE...

...IF **ONE** ROGUE CAN FIND HIS WAY THERE, SO MAY **ANOTHER!** ANOTHER MORE WILLING TO DELIVER SOLO'S HIDE **WITHOUT** WASTING MY TIME!

Meanwhile...

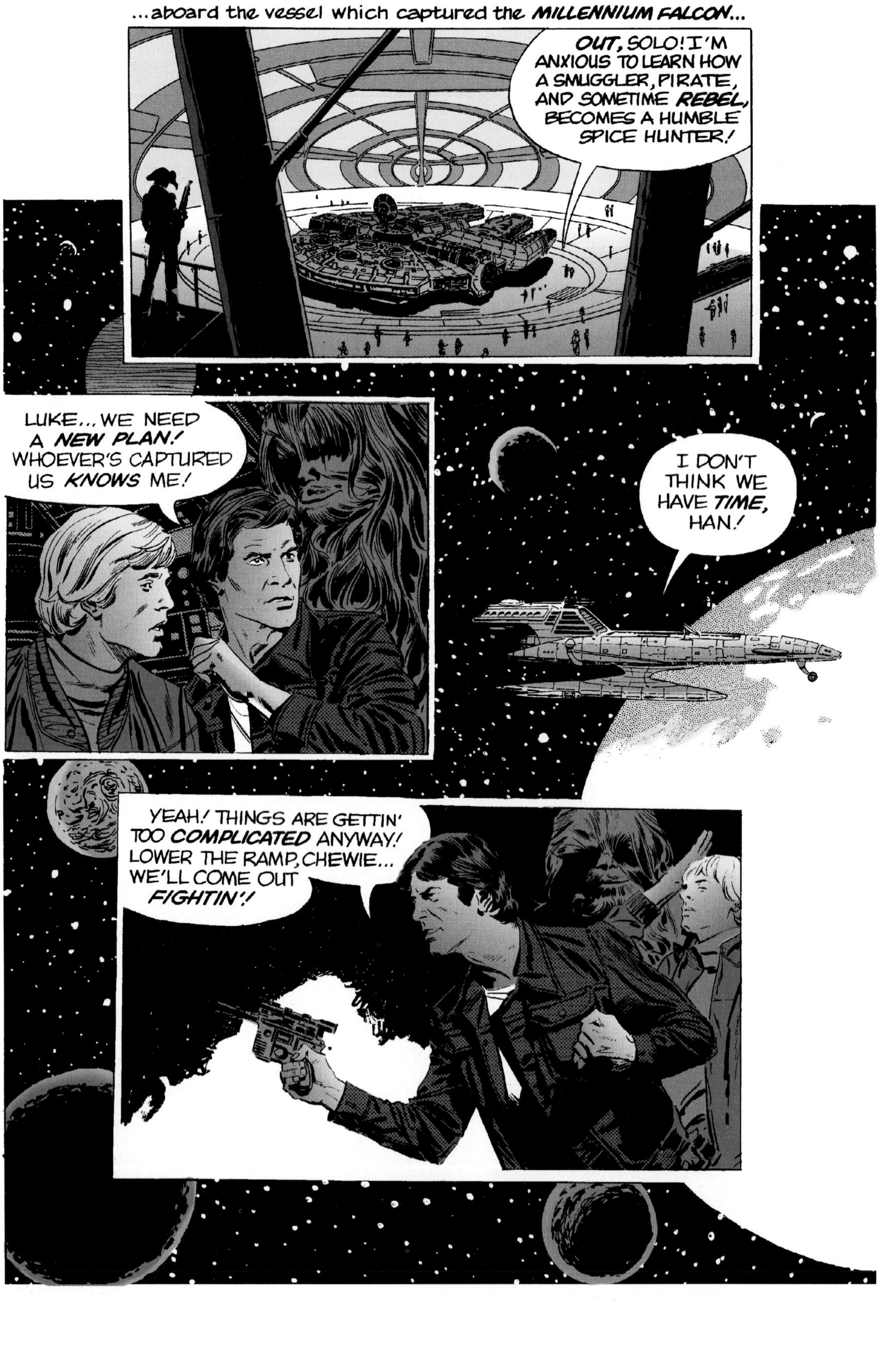
...aboard the vessel which captured the MILLENNIUM FALCON...
OUT, SOLO! I'M ANXIOUS TO LEARN HOW A SMUGGLER, PIRATE, AND SOMETIME REBEL, BECOMES A HUMBLE SPICE HUNTER!
LUKE... WE NEED A NEW PLAN! WHOEVER'S CAPTURED US KNOWS ME!
I DON'T THINK WE HAVE TIME, HAN!
YEAH! THINGS ARE GETTIN' TOO COMPLICATED ANYWAY! LOWER THE RAMP, CHEWIE... WE'LL COME OUT FIGHTIN'!

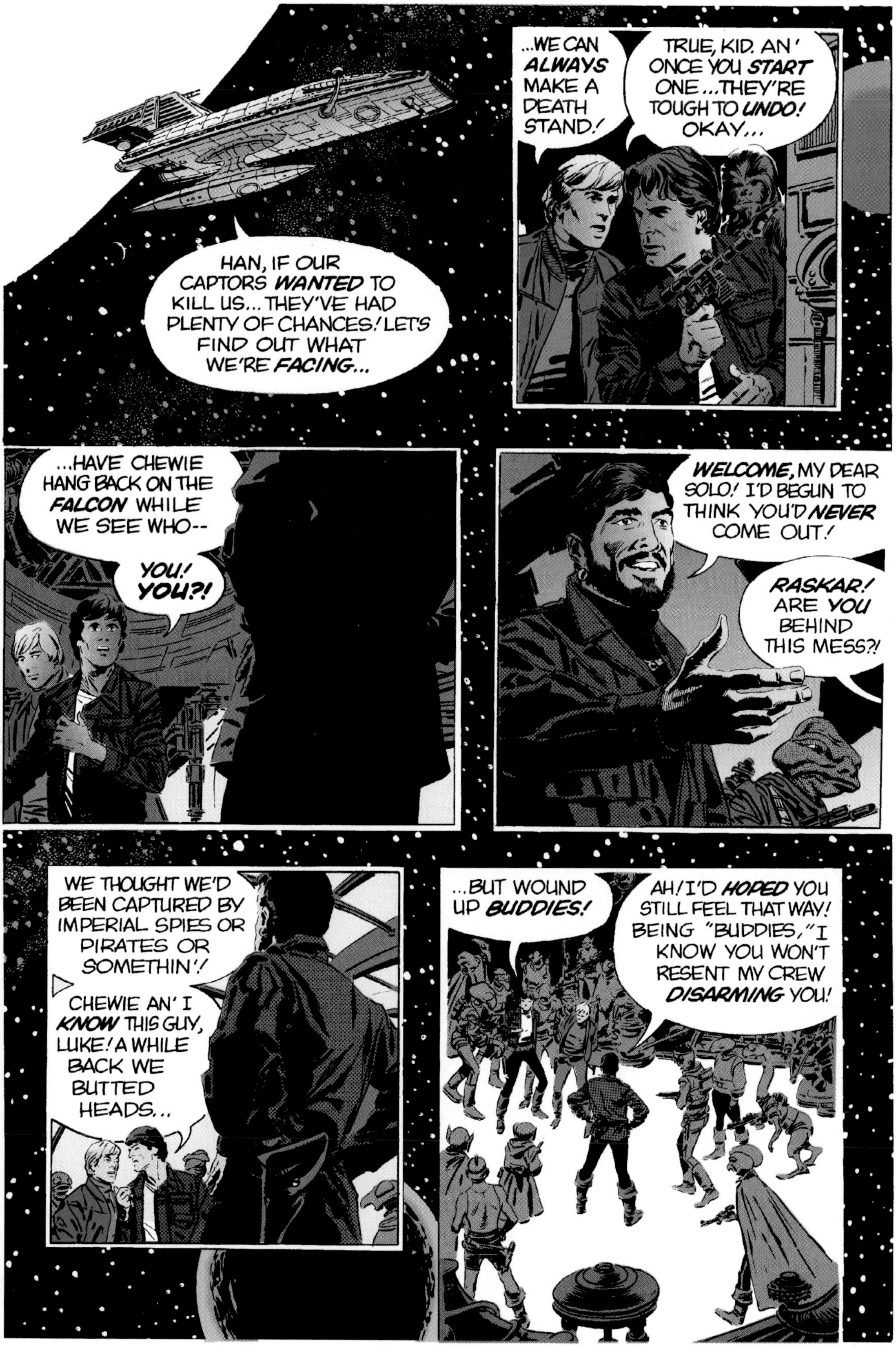
HAN, IF OUR CAPTORS WANTED TO KILL US... THEY'VE HAD PLENTY OF CHANCES! LET'S FIND OUT WHAT WE'RE FACING...
...WE CAN ALWAYS MAKE A DEATH STAND!
TRUE, KID. AN' ONCE YOU START ONE... THEY'RE TOUGH TO UNDO! OKAY...
...HAVE CHEWIE HANG BACK ON THE FALCON WHILE WE SEE WHO--
YOU! YOU?!
WELCOME, MY DEAR SOLO! I'D BEGUN TO THINK YOU'D NEVER COME OUT!
RASKAR! ARE YOU BEHIND THIS MESS?!
WE THOUGHT WE'D BEEN CAPTURED BY IMPERIAL SPIES OR PIRATES OR SOMETHIN'!
CHEWIE AN' I KNOW THIS GUY, LUKE! A WHILE BACK WE BUTTED HEADS...
...BUT WOUND UP BUDDIES!
AH! I'D HOPED YOU STILL FEEL THAT WAY! BEING "BUDDIES," I KNOW YOU WON'T RESENT MY CREW DISARMING YOU!

RASKAR, WHAT *IS* THIS?! I *HELPED* YOU THE LAST TIME WE MET!

AND I *APPRECIATED* IT, MY DEAR SOLO! EVEN SO... MY FORTUNES TOOK A TURN FOR THE WORSE!

INSTEAD OF RULING A MODEST PLANET, AS WHEN YOU MET ME... I'M REDUCED TO BEING A *PIRATE* AGAIN!

HAN... THAT'S *ONE* OF THE THINGS WE FEARED!

CHEWIE'S STILL ON THE *FALCON*, LUKE... HE'LL BLOW 'ER UP BEFORE LETTIN' PIRATES STEAL HER!

WE DON'T WANT YOUR *SHIP*, OLD FRIEND... WE WANT *YOU!*

SEE THE WOOKIEE DOESN'T *LEAVE* THE *MILLENNIUM FALCON*... BUT DO NOTHING TO MAKE HIM ACT *RASHLY!*

WHAT ABOUT *LUKE* AND ME, RASKAR?

WHY, NOW THAT YOU'RE DISARMED, MY DEAR SOLO, WE CAN ADJOURN TO MY CABIN FOR DRINKS...

...AND A CIVILIZED DISCUSSION OF MY INTENTION TO *SELL* YOU TO JABBA THE HUTT!

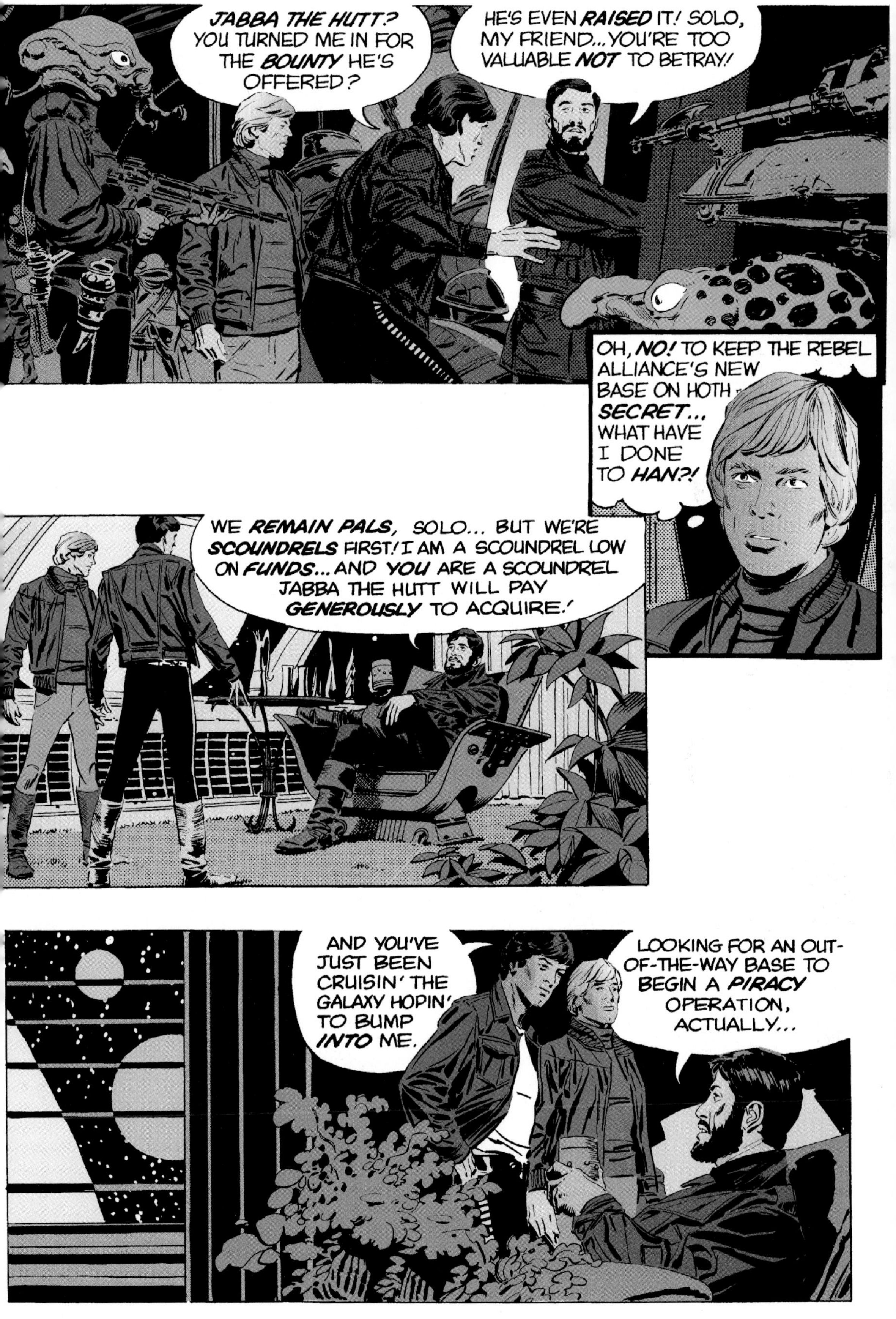
JABBA THE HUTT? YOU TURNED ME IN FOR THE BOUNTY HE'S OFFERED?
HE'S EVEN RAISED IT! SOLO, MY FRIEND... YOU'RE TOO VALUABLE NOT TO BETRAY!
OH, NO! TO KEEP THE REBEL ALLIANCE'S NEW BASE ON HOTH SECRET... WHAT HAVE I DONE TO HAN?!
WE REMAIN PALS, SOLO... BUT WE'RE SCOUNDRELS FIRST! I AM A SCOUNDREL LOW ON FUNDS... AND YOU ARE A SCOUNDREL JABBA THE HUTT WILL PAY GENEROUSLY TO ACQUIRE!
AND YOU'VE JUST BEEN CRUISIN' THE GALAXY HOPIN' TO BUMP INTO ME.
LOOKING FOR AN OUT-OF-THE-WAY BASE TO BEGIN A PIRACY OPERATION, ACTUALLY...

...AND SPOTTED *YOUR* SHIP.' NOW... JABBA'S BOUNTY IS *MINE!* UNLESS, PERHAPS...YOU HAVE A *COUNTERPROPOSAL?*

HAN! WHAT ABOUT YOUR *REWARD* FROM PRINCESS LEIA?

KID, ARE YOU *NUTS?!* YOU'RE BAITIN' THIS PIRATE WITH SOMETHIN' I DON'T *HAVE* ANYMORE.'

IGNORE *SKYWALKER* HERE, RASKAR.' TENSE SITUATIONS MAKE HIM BABBLE A BIT, IMAGINE STUFF.' YOU KNOW... *LIE!*

YOUNG SKYWALKER IS *NOT* LYING, MY DEAR SOLO! SINCE RESUMING MY CAREER AS A PIRATE, I'VE HEARD *PERSISTENT* RUMORS OF YOUR AIDING THE REBEL ALLIANCE...

...AND BEING *WELL REWARDED* FOR IT! SINCE YOU HAVEN'T HAD OPPORTUNITY TO *SPEND* SUCH WEALTH...YOU MUST HAVE *HIDDEN* IT!

RASKAR, OL' BUDDY...

...YOU GONNA BELIEVE *RUMORS*... OR *ME*?

WHICHEVER MAKES ME *WEALTHIEST*, MY FRIEND! IT'S TIME TO *RECONSIDER* YOUR POSITION!

I'M TRYING TO *AVOID* SELLING YOU FOR JABBA'S BOUNTY! BUT IF YOU'RE GOING TO BE STUBBORN...

...THINGS COULD GET *NASTY!*

HAN, YOUR TREASURE IS OBVIOUSLY WHAT RASKAR'S BEEN *FISHING* FOR ALL ALONG... *GIVE* IT TO HIM!

KID, I CAN'T GIVE WHAT I DON'T *HAVE!*

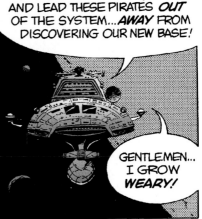

BUT WE CAN *PRETEND,* HAN... AND LEAD THESE PIRATES *OUT* OF THE SYSTEM....*AWAY* FROM DISCOVERING OUR NEW BASE!

GENTLEMEN... I GROW *WEARY!*

...ORD MANTELL!

AH, SOLO... YOU *NEVER* DISAPPOINT ME! SINCE YOU ARE *KNOWN* TO FREQUENT THERE, IT'S A MOST *BELIEVABLE* HIDING SPOT...

OKAY, *OKAY,* RASKAR! LUKE AN' I HAVE TALKED THIS OVER...I'LL *TELL* YOU WHERE I HID MY REWARD FROM PRINCESS LEIA! ON...UH...

...AND, OF COURSE, *TOTAL FICTION!*

YOU MAY *RECALL,* MY DEAR SOLO... I LIKE TO STAY IN CONDITION BY *PRACTICING* WITH THIS PRIMITIVE WEAPON! I'M *QUITE* GOOD!

...BUT *IMPATIENCE* MAKES ME SLIP! AND WHEN I'VE WATCHED YOUR SHIP TRAVEL TO A FORSAKEN PLANET IN AN OBSCURE SYSTEM *PERFECT* FOR HIDING TREASURE...

...ONLY TO BE TOLD THAT TREASURE'S SUPPOSEDLY ON ORD MANTELL, I GROW *MOST* IMPATIENT! ONE MIGHT THINK YOU WERE TRYING TO LURE US *AWAY* FROM HERE!

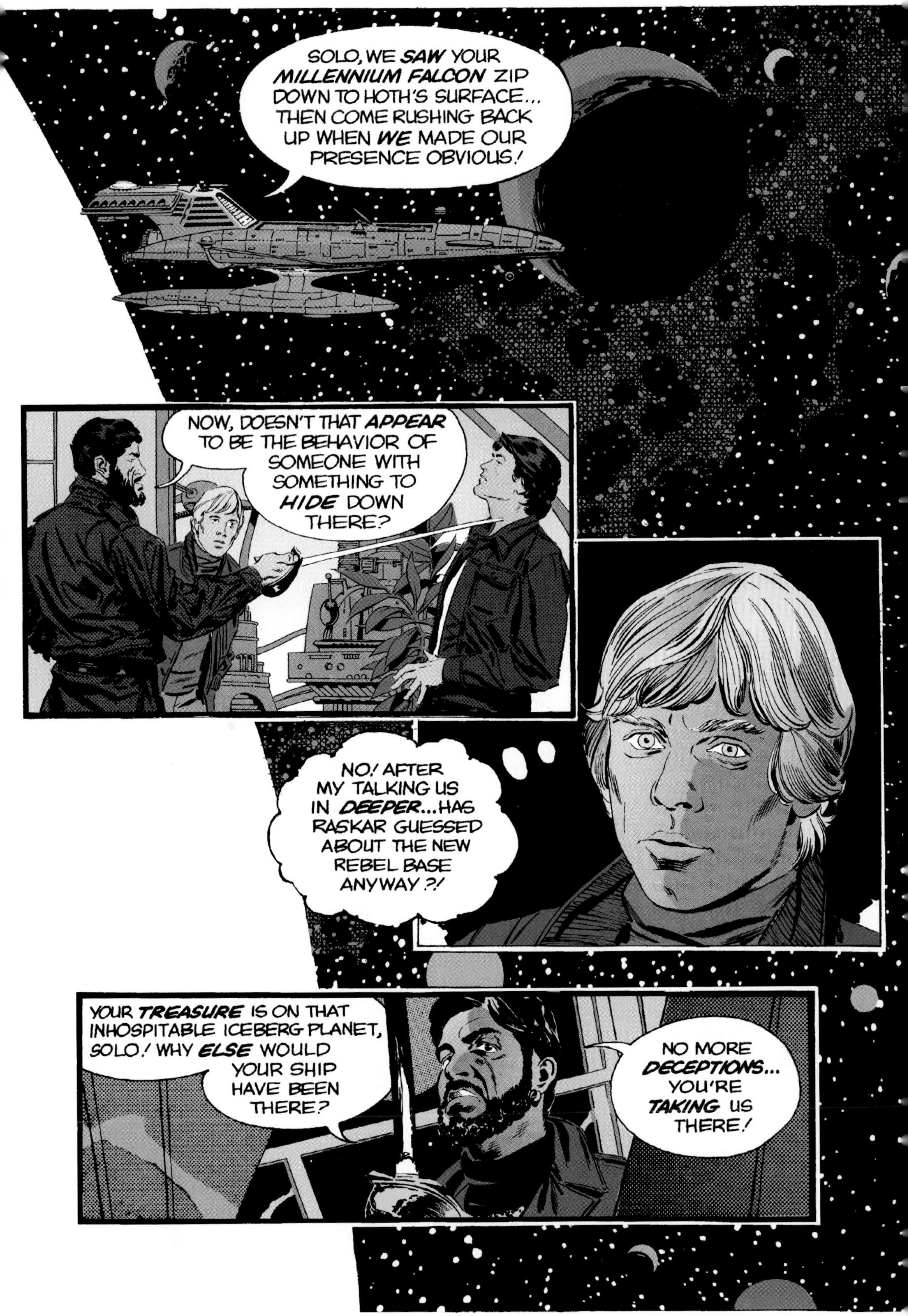
SOLO, WE SAW YOUR MILLENNIUM FALCON ZIP DOWN TO HOTH'S SURFACE... THEN COME RUSHING BACK UP WHEN WE MADE OUR PRESENCE OBVIOUS!
NOW, DOESN'T THAT APPEAR TO BE THE BEHAVIOR OF SOMEONE WITH SOMETHING TO HIDE DOWN THERE?
NO! AFTER MY TALKING US IN DEEPER...HAS RASKAR GUESSED ABOUT THE NEW REBEL BASE ANYWAY?!
YOUR TREASURE IS ON THAT INHOSPITABLE ICEBERG PLANET, SOLO! WHY ELSE WOULD YOUR SHIP HAVE BEEN THERE?
NO MORE DECEPTIONS... YOU'RE TAKING US THERE!

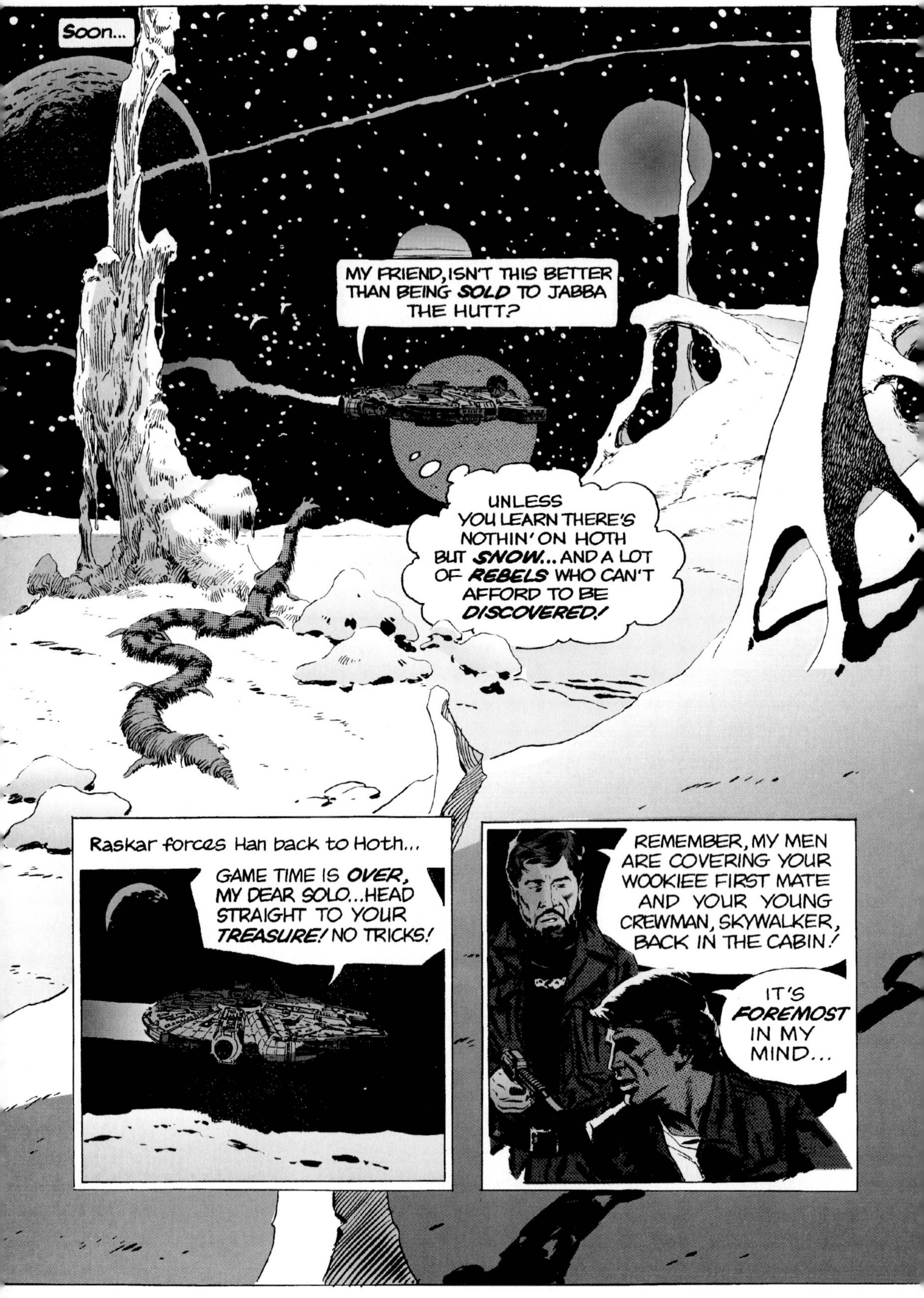
Soon...
MY FRIEND, ISN'T THIS BETTER THAN BEING SOLD TO JABBA THE HUTT?
UNLESS YOU LEARN THERE'S NOTHIN' ON HOTH BUT SNOW... AND A LOT OF REBELS WHO CAN'T AFFORD TO BE DISCOVERED!
Raskar forces Han back to Hoth...
GAME TIME IS OVER, MY DEAR SOLO...HEAD STRAIGHT TO YOUR TREASURE! NO TRICKS!
REMEMBER, MY MEN ARE COVERING YOUR WOOKIEE FIRST MATE AND YOUR YOUNG CREWMAN, SKYWALKER, BACK IN THE CABIN!
IT'S FOREMOST IN MY MIND...

...ALONG WITH THE FACT THAT I'M RUNNING OUT OF IDEAS TO *STALL* THIS PIRATE FROM DISCOVERING MY "TREASURE" DOESN'T *EXIST!*

SOLO, WE'RE MOVING TOWARD HOTH'S *EQUATOR!* THAT'S *NOT* WHERE YOU WERE HEADED WHEN WE ORIGINALLY SPOTTED THE *MILLENNIUM FALCON!*

YOU *KNOW* I'M DEVIOUS, RASKAR...

...I NEVER HEAD STRAIGHT FOR *ANYTHING!* UNLESS I'M FORCED TO...LIKE *NOW!*

PARTICULARLY WHEN I'M TRYING TO *HIDE* THAT THERE'S A *REBEL BASE* HERE!

IF WE'RE HEADED *STRAIGHT* FOR YOUR TREASURE...WHY IS IT *TAKING* SO LONG? I ADMIRE YOU IMMENSELY, DEAR FELLOW...BUT DON'T *TRUST* YOU FOR AN INSTANT!

MY PATIENCE IS WEARING *THIN,* SOLO! IF YOU CAN'T PRODUCE THAT TREASURE--AND *SOON*-- THERE'S ALWAYS JABBA THE HUTT'S *BOUNTY!*

RASKAR...

...WHAT'S THE USE IN *HIDIN'* SOMETHIN' UNLESS YOU HIDE IT *WELL?* DON'T WORRY...THE SPOT'S COMIN' UP *SOON*...

...I *HOPE!*

HANG *ON,* RASKAR! HERE'S WHAT I'VE BEEN *LOOKING* FOR!

SOLO, YOU WOULDN'T BE *MAD* ENOUGH TO HIDE TREASURE IN--

SOLO!

Han plunges the *MILLENNIUM FALCON* into the ravine's depths!

THIS IS A *TRICK,* SOLO! NO ONE WOULD HIDE TREASURE IN THIS *CHASM!* I'LL--

TEMPER, RASKAR...

...IT'S NOT THE TIME TO MAKE YOUR PILOT *NERVOUS!*

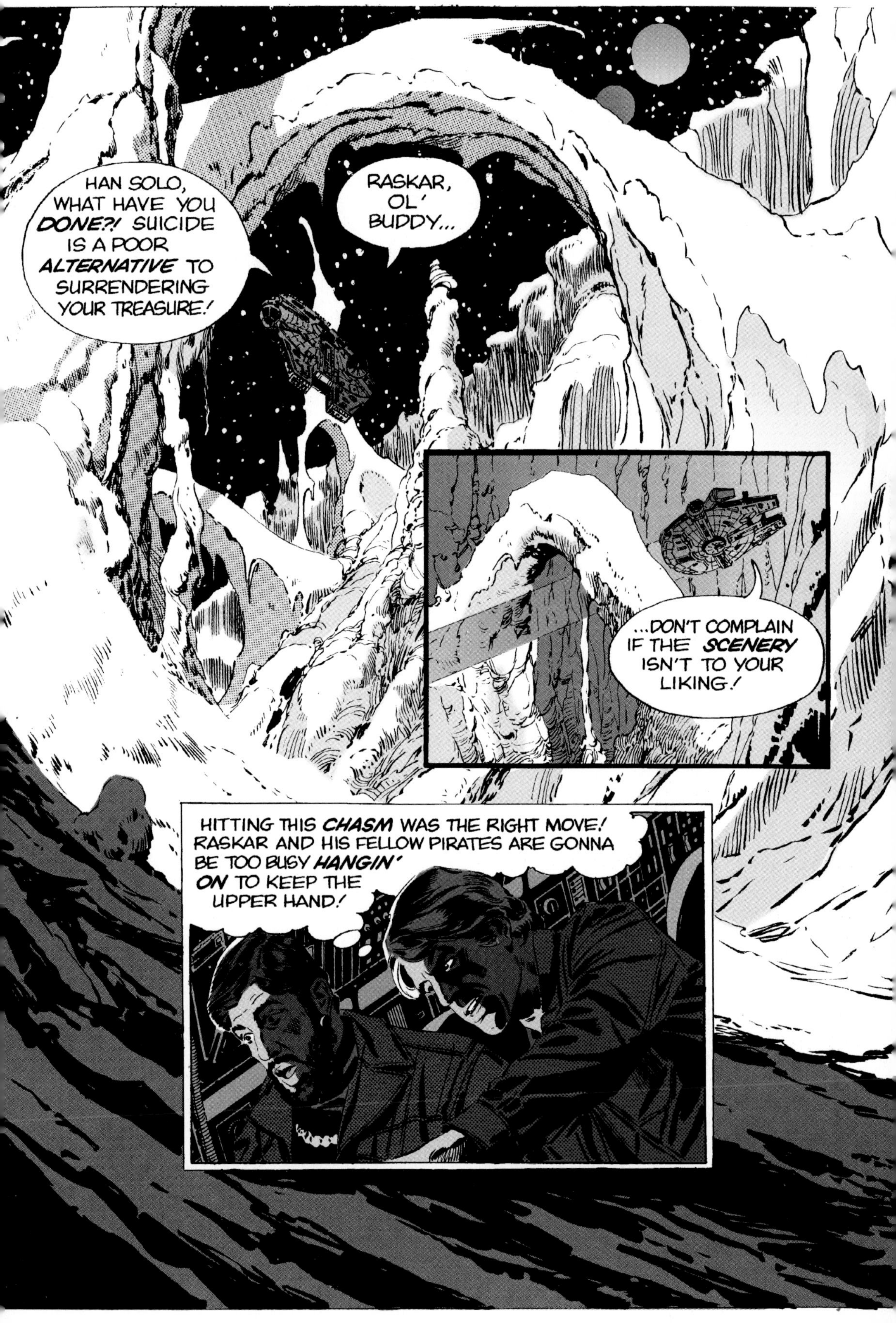
HAN SOLO, WHAT HAVE YOU DONE?! SUICIDE IS A POOR ALTERNATIVE TO SURRENDERING YOUR TREASURE!
RASKAR, OL' BUDDY...
...DON'T COMPLAIN IF THE SCENERY ISN'T TO YOUR LIKING!
HITTING THIS CHASM WAS THE RIGHT MOVE! RASKAR AND HIS FELLOW PIRATES ARE GONNA BE TOO BUSY HANGIN' ON TO KEEP THE UPPER HAND!

IF LUKE AN' CHEWIE CAN GRAB THE BUNCH COVERIN' *THEM* WHILE I TAKE CARE OF--

SOLO, WHERE'S YOUR *MIND?!* THIS PIT IS A *DEAD END!*

NO SHIP CAN GO THROUGH THESE *MAD* MANEUVERS WITHOUT RISK OF A *STALL!*

SHIPS HAVE *IMPROVED* SINCE YOU *LAST* WENT PIRATING, RASKAR...

...AND THE *FALCON'S* ONE OF THE BEST! SO YOU CAN *FORGET* ABOUT...

SOLO! I CAN'T *HEAR* THE ENGINES! W-WHAT--?!

I THINK MAYBE WE JUST *STALLED!*

Without power, the *MILLENNIUM FALCON* hurtles back toward the chasm floor...

...as Han fights to reignite her engines from the stall...

COME ON, BABY! COME ON!

...in time for **SOME** sort of landing!

The **FALCON** plows to a halt along the **BOTTOM** of the deep ravine! The noise of its desperate landing still echoes up the icy walls...

...and the **INTENSITY** of the sound shatters **MORE** than the stillness!

A **HATCH** opens atop the **MILLENNIUM FALCON**...

GUESS I'M THE ONLY ONE NOT **STUNNED!** IF THERE'S NO SERIOUS DAMAGE TO THE **SHIP**, I CAN--

AW... NO!

ICE SLIDE!!

BLAST IT! DID I SUCCESSFULLY BRING US DOWN AFTER STALLING...

...JUST TO GET BURIED ALIVE?!

I HOPE NOT, SOLO...

...MY MEN BACK IN THE CABIN ARE ALREADY IN THE MOOD TO BEGIN BLASTING SKYWALKER AND THE WOOKIEE! I'M NOT FAR BEHIND REGARDING YOU!

EASY, SOUNDS LIKE IT'S STOPPING.

And...

LUCKY! MOST OF IT MISSED US! BUT I'D FORGET USIN' BLASTERS, OL' BUDDY... NEXT LOUD NOISE COULD COLLAPSE THE WHOLE RAVINE!

SOLO...WE CAN'T TAKE OFF WITHOUT MAKING NOISE!

YOU'VE *TRAPPED* US IN THIS RAVINE, YOU CORELLIAN CRACKPOT!

HEY, *I* DIDN'T WANT TO RETURN TO HOTH... YOU *ORDERED* ME!

I ORDERED YOU TO TAKE ME TO YOUR *TREASURE*, SOLO... I'M BEGINNING TO *DOUBT* YOU EVER HAD ONE!

WATCH THAT *KNIFE!*

IT'S A *SWORD*, MY EX-FRIEND, AND IT'S ABOUT TO PIERCE YOUR *GIZZARD!*

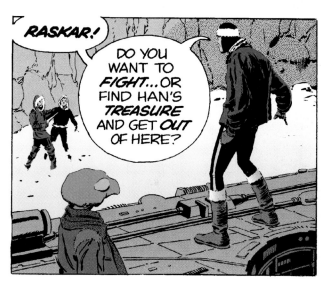

RASKAR!

DO YOU WANT TO *FIGHT*... OR FIND HAN'S *TREASURE* AND GET *OUT* OF HERE?

LUKE... YOU KNOW SOMETHING WE DON'T?

RASKAR'S THUGS LET ME TRY THE *COMMUNICATOR.*

YOUR PIRATE SHIP'S NOT SO BIG THAT IT CAN'T COME DOWN INTO THE ATMOSPHERE IF SUMMONED, RASKAR... AND USE ITS *TRACTOR BEAM* TO PULL US OUT!

MY DEAR SOLO, THIS LAD HAS MORE *POTENTIAL* THAN I'D *EXPECT* OF SOMEONE TRAINED BY YOU!

THERE'S *STILL* A PROBLEM!

THESE CANYON WALLS INTERFERE WITH *TRANSMISSION*, RASKAR! I COULDN'T RAISE YOUR SHIP!

THEN... WE'RE STILL *TRAPPED!*

MAYBE *NOT!* I TRIED THE *FALCON'S SCANNERS* AS WELL AS THE *COMMUNICATOR...*

THAT WALL AT THE END OF THE CANYON ISN'T AS *THICK* AS IT LOOKS! THERE ARE *CAVERNS* BEHIND IT!

I THOUGHT YOU WERE A *SHARP* PIRATE LEADER! WHERE DO YOU THINK HAN'S *TREASURE* IS?!

OH, *NO!* KID... WHAT ARE YOU GETTING US INTO *NOW?!*

GET EVERYONE TO START *DIGGING!* THOSE CAVERNS COULD LEAD US *OUT* OF HERE, RASKAR!

OR INTO SOMETHING *WORSE*, SKYWALKER! I'M *WEARY* OF YOU TWO LEADING US ON!

EVERYONE...WE'VE *DIGGING* TO DO! FOR ESCAPE...AND FOR *TREASURE!*

KID, THEY'LL *SLAUGHTER* US FOR MAKIN' 'EM WORK, THEN COME UP *EMPTY-HANDED!*

DON'T WORRY, HAN...I'VE GOT A *PLAN!*

YEAH...THAT'S HOW ALL THIS *STARTED!*

RASKAR! SKYWALKER'S *RIGHT!* THIS WALL *ISN'T* SO THICK... WE'RE BREAKING THROUGH TO A *CAVERN!*

JUST WHAT THE *SCANNERS* INDICATED! IF WE CAN FIND OUR WAY TO THE SURFACE--

A COMSET WILL *WORK* THERE WITHOUT THE *INTERFERENCE* IT GETS DOWN HERE. BUT...

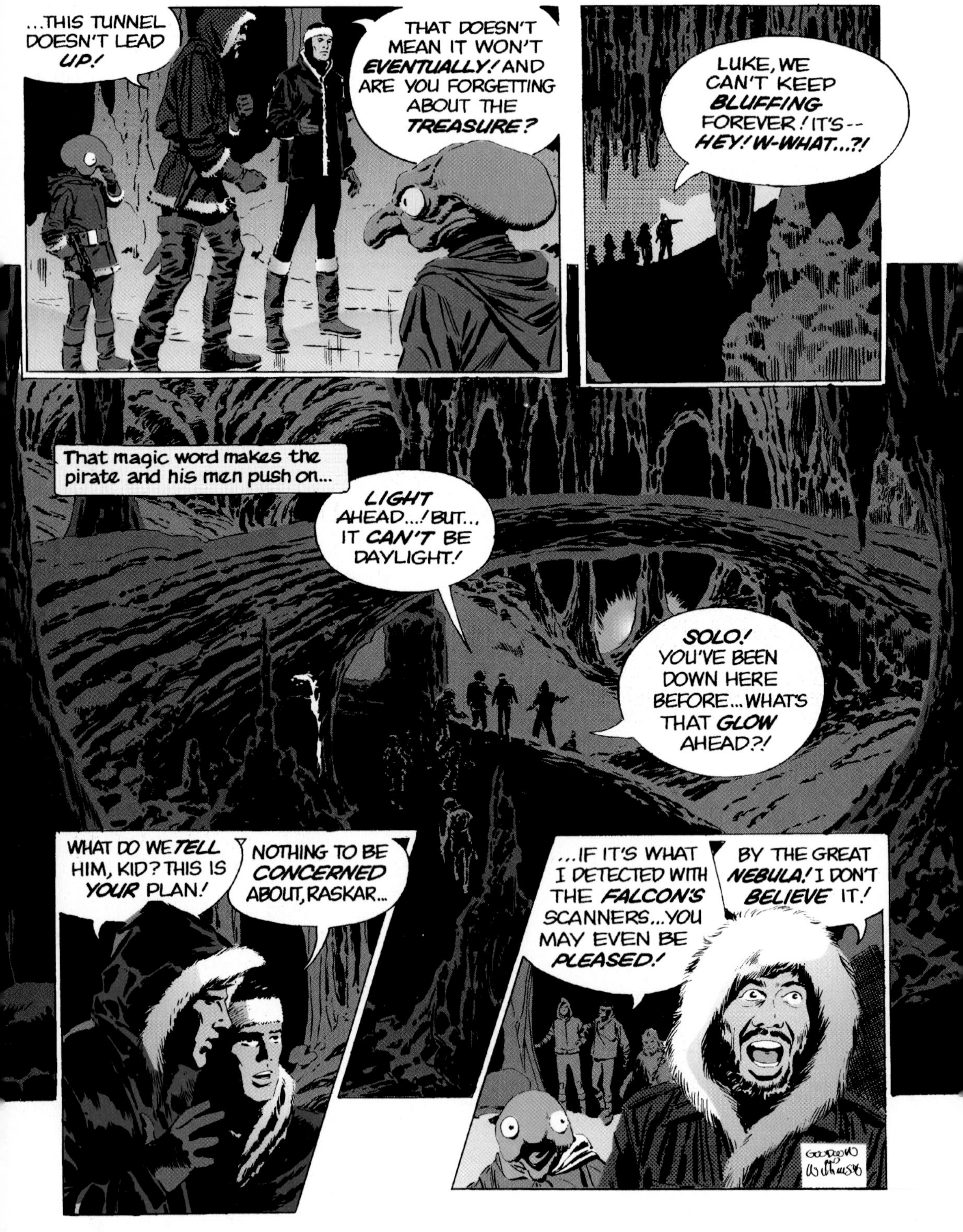
...THIS TUNNEL DOESN'T LEAD UP!
THAT DOESN'T MEAN IT WON'T EVENTUALLY! AND ARE YOU FORGETTING ABOUT THE TREASURE?
LUKE, WE CAN'T KEEP BLUFFING FOREVER! IT'S-- HEY! W-WHAT...?!
That magic word makes the pirate and his men push on...
LIGHT AHEAD...! BUT... IT CAN'T BE DAYLIGHT!
SOLO! YOU'VE BEEN DOWN HERE BEFORE...WHAT'S THAT GLOW AHEAD?!
WHAT DO WE TELL HIM, KID? THIS IS YOUR PLAN!
NOTHING TO BE CONCERNED ABOUT, RASKAR...
...IF IT'S WHAT I DETECTED WITH THE FALCON'S SCANNERS...YOU MAY EVEN BE PLEASED!
BY THE GREAT NEBULA! I DON'T BELIEVE IT!

OUR STORY CONCLUDES

NUNIS · 94

LUMNI-SPICE! A PIRATE'S *DREAM!*

RAREST FORM OF SPICE IN THE *GALAXY,* RIGHT, RASKAR? BARELY HAS TO BE *MINED!*

LUKE, YOU PICKED UP ON THE *FALCON'S* SCANNERS THAT THIS STUFF WAS IN HERE?

"COULDN'T *BELIEVE* OUR LUCK, HAN! A TREASURE...RIGHT WHEN WE *NEEDED* IT!"

KID, I WISH YOU'D *TOLD* ME! IF THIS IS *LUCK*... IT'S ALL *BAD!*

THE REBELS PAID YOU OFF IN *LUMNI-SPICE*, MY DEAR SOLO? YOU MUST HAVE DONE THEM A *MONUMENTAL* SERVICE!

I'M A *HANDY* GUY, RASKAR.

AND YOU SET IT GROWING IN THIS OUT-OF-THE-WAY *CAVERN* ON HOTH TO *INCREASE* YOUR FORTUNE?

THAT'S ME... *GREEDY.* RIGHT?

HAN, I DON'T SEE WHY FINDING THIS STUFF IS *BAD LUCK!*

KID... I'M PRAYIN' *NONE* OF US SEE IT!

WHAT *IS* IT ABOUT LUMNI-SPICE? I DON'T *UNDERSTAND!*

COMIN' FROM A *FARM* WORLD, YOU *COULDN'T,* LUKE. LET'S GET *CHEWIE* AND I'LL--*NO!* TOO LATE!

THE THING THAT MAKES LUMNI-SPICE SO *RARE*--TO SAY NOTHIN' OF *DIFFICULT* TO HARVEST--IS THAT IT'S THE FAVORITE *FOOD* FOR *DRAGON-SLUGS,* LUKE! ALMOST *NOBODY* LIVES TO HARVEST IT!

HAN, WHEN I SPOTTED THE *SPICE CACHE* ON THE *FALCON'S* SCANNERS...I DIDN'T *KNOW!*

Raskar's hardbitten pirates react quickly, but their blaster fire has small effect...

...except for the reverberations *SHAKING* the cavern ceiling!

THE SHOOTING'S BRINGING DOWN PART OF THE *CAVERN ROOF!* IT'LL *BURY* THAT THING!

NO, LUKE! THE REASON THEY CALL 'EM *DRAGON-*SLUGS...

...IS THAT THEY BREATHE *FIRE!*

RASKAR'S FALLEN IN ITS PATH!

YEAH! THAT PIRATE HASN'T HAD THE *EXPERIENCE* RUNNIN' FROM MONSTERS *WE* HAVE, LUKE! LET'S *GO!*

HAN, WE *CAN'T* LEAVE HIM! AT LEAST *I* WON'T!

WHEN HE ISN'T TRYIN' TO *SELL* ME TO JABBA THE HUTT... RASKAR'S NOT A *BAD GUY*, LUKE!

BUT SAVIN' HIM *NOW*...

...MEANS GOIN' UP AGAINST A FLAME-SPEWING *DRAGON-SLUG* UNARMED!

WE'RE *NOT* UNARMED, HAN! I'VE BEEN *SAVING* SOMETHING...

...FOR THE RIGHT MOMENT!

YOUR *LIGHTSABER!* LUKE... *HOW?* RASKAR *TOOK* ALL OUR WEAPONS WHEN HE *CAPTURED* US!

I *HID* IT ON THE *FALCON* BEFORE WE SURRENDERED, HAN...

...AND *GRABBED* IT AGAIN AFTER WE TRAVELED HERE! I FIGURED ON USING IT WHEN THE *TIME* WAS RIGHT.

THAT LOOKS LIKE *NOW!*

THE BEST *JEDI KNIGHT* COULDN'T FIGHT A DRAGON-SLUG *AND* HAUL RASKAR TO SAFETY!

C'MON, CHEWIE! THE TROUBLE WITH HAVIN' *FRIENDS* WHO PLAY THE HERO...

...IS THAT SOONER OR LATER THEY SUCK *YOU* INTO DOING IT *TOO!*

WITH THAT MONSTER SPEWIN' *FIRE*...LUKE CAN'T GET *CLOSE* ENOUGH TO USE HIS LIGHTSABER! GOTTA *DISTRACT* IT SOMEHOW! BUT--

WOWRRRRRAAGH!

CHEWIE! THAT'S *TOO MUCH* DISTRACTIN'... IT'LL TURN ITS FLAME ON *US!*

CHEWIE, YOU BIG GOOF! I *WARNED* YOU THAT THING'D TURN ON US! BUT *BELIEVE* ME...

...THERE'S *NO SATISFACTION* IN BEIN' RIGHT!

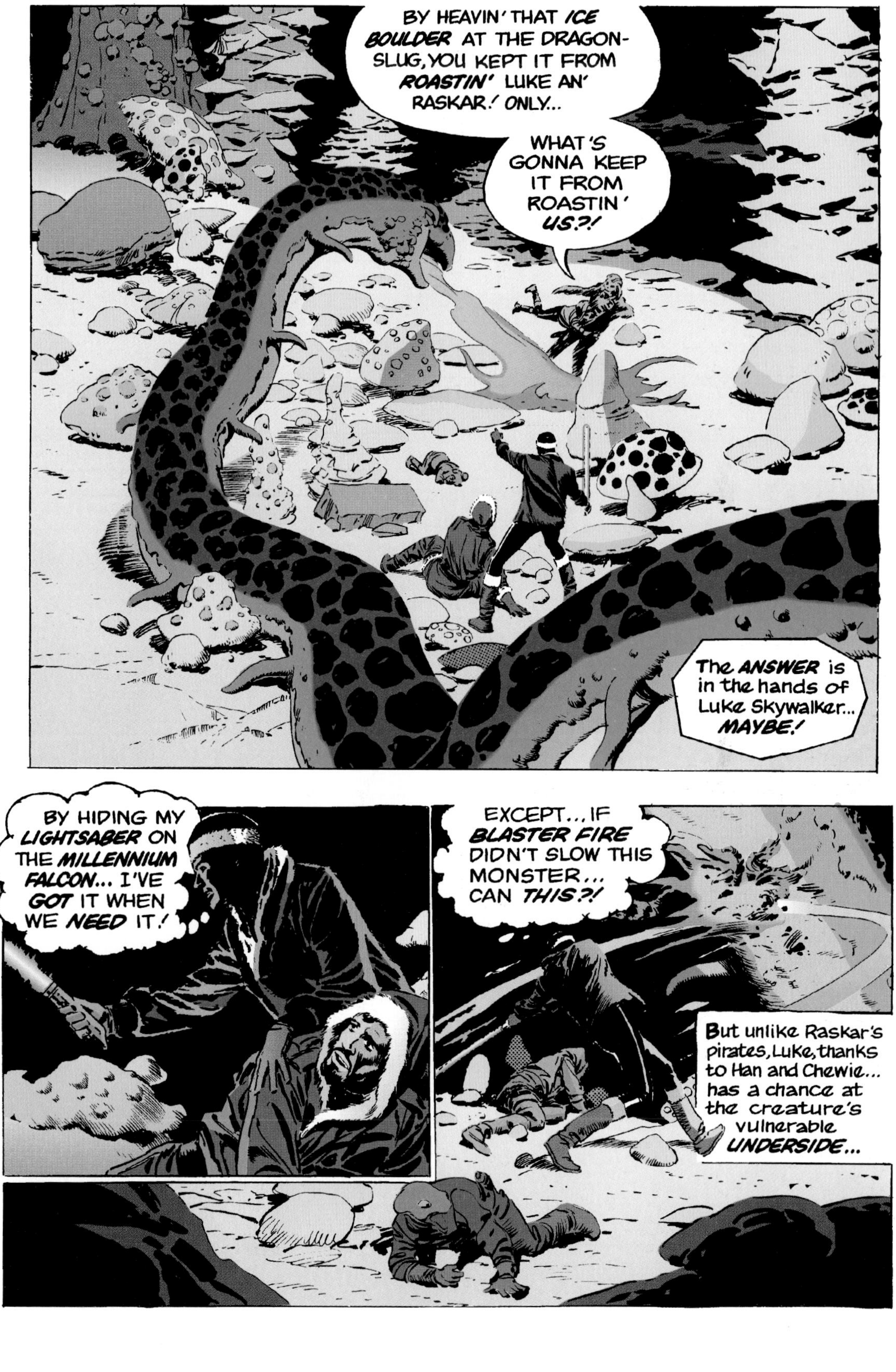

BY HEAVIN' THAT ICE BOULDER AT THE DRAGON-SLUG, YOU KEPT IT FROM ROASTIN' LUKE AN' RASKAR! ONLY...
WHAT'S GONNA KEEP IT FROM ROASTIN' US?!
The ANSWER is in the hands of Luke Skywalker... MAYBE!
BY HIDING MY LIGHTSABER ON THE MILLENNIUM FALCON... I'VE GOT IT WHEN WE NEED IT!
EXCEPT... IF BLASTER FIRE DIDN'T SLOW THIS MONSTER... CAN THIS?!
But unlike Raskar's pirates, Luke, thanks to Han and Chewie... has a chance at the creature's vulnerable UNDERSIDE...

...and strikes there *AGAIN* and *AGAIN!*

VAAROWWWWRKK!

RIGHT, CHEWIE! IT'S *HURT* OR IT WOULDN'T BE REARIN' UP LIKE THAT! BUT EVEN IF IT'S *DYIN'*... IT'LL *CRUSH* 'EM WHEN IT *FALLS!*

WITH SOMETHIN' *THAT* BIG...EVEN THE *DEATH THROES* CAN KILL YA!

And the creature topples... *TOWARD* Luke and Raskar!

As the falling carcass of the dragon-slug threatens to *CRUSH* Luke and Raskar...

MOVE, CHEWIE... IT'S GONNA BE *CLOSE!*

Perhaps... *TOO* close!

For a time, *STILLNESS* fills the Lumni-spice cavern. Then...

RASKAR, IF YOU WERE ANY *HEAVIER* OR IF THIS MONSTER FELL ANY *FASTER*...

...WE'D BE *UNDER* THE DRAGON-SLUG INSTEAD.

YOU HAVE *SAVED* US, SOLO, MY FRIEND... BUT ONLY *TEMPORARILY*, I FEAR!

HEY! YOU'RE *ALIVE* THANKS TO US, AN' YOU'RE STILL *COMPLAININ'*, YOU PIRATE?!

FIGHTING THE DRAGON-SLUG CAUSED *COLLAPSE*, SOLO... *LOOK!* THAT'S *BLOCKED* THE ENTRANCE!

WE'RE *TRAPPED* IN THIS CAVERN... UNTIL THE *REST* OF IT COLLAPSES!

MAYBE *NOT!* HAN! CHEWIE! RASKAR! COME BACK *THIS* WAY... I'VE GOT AN *IDEA!*

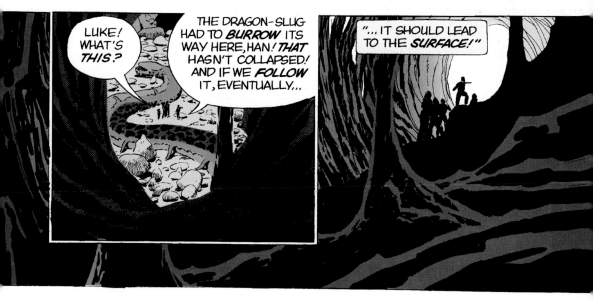

LUKE! WHAT'S *THIS?*

THE DRAGON-SLUG HAD TO *BURROW* ITS WAY HERE, HAN! *THAT* HASN'T COLLAPSED! AND IF WE *FOLLOW* IT, EVENTUALLY...

"...IT SHOULD LEAD TO THE *SURFACE!*"

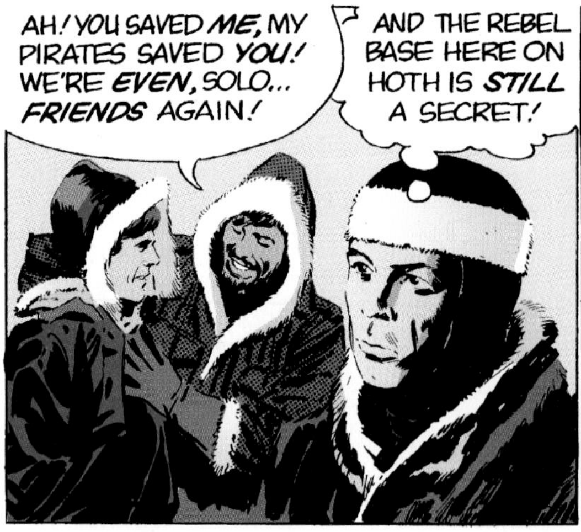
AH! YOU SAVED *ME*, MY PIRATES SAVED *YOU!* WE'RE *EVEN*, SOLO... *FRIENDS* AGAIN!
AND THE REBEL BASE HERE ON HOTH IS *STILL* A SECRET!

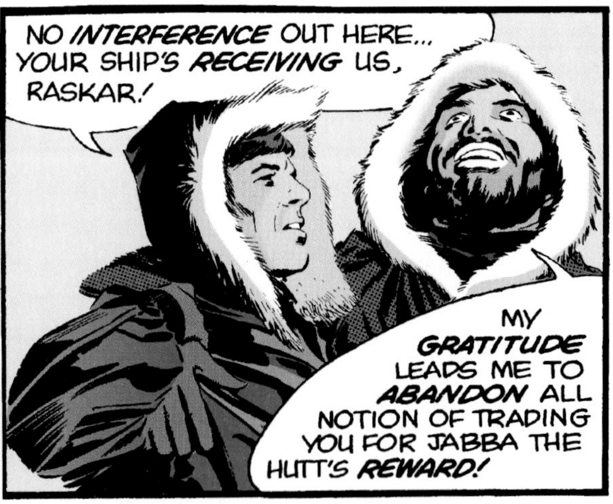
NO *INTERFERENCE* OUT HERE... YOUR SHIP'S *RECEIVING* US, RASKAR!
MY *GRATITUDE* LEADS ME TO *ABANDON* ALL NOTION OF TRADING YOU FOR JABBA THE HUTT'S *REWARD!*

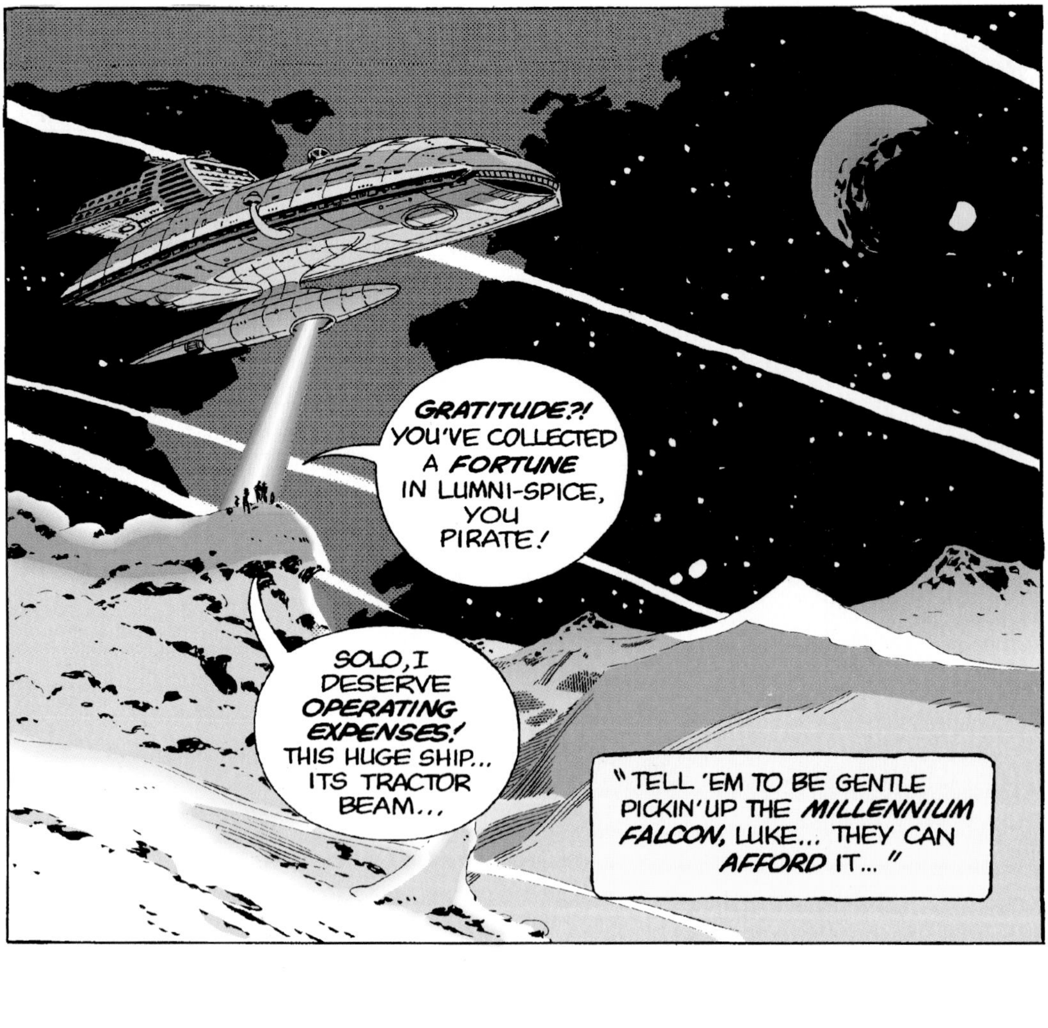
GRATITUDE?! YOU'VE COLLECTED A *FORTUNE* IN LUMNI-SPICE, YOU PIRATE!
SOLO, I DESERVE *OPERATING EXPENSES!* THIS HUGE SHIP... ITS TRACTOR BEAM...
"TELL 'EM TO BE GENTLE PICKIN' UP THE *MILLENNIUM FALCON,* LUKE... THEY CAN *AFFORD* IT..."

"WITH ALL THE *LUMNI-SPICE* THIS PIRATE'S TAKIN' AWAY... IT'S GONNA BE THE BEST-PAID *TOW JOB* IN THE HISTORY OF THE GALAXY!"

RASK, OL' BUDDY... WE HAD A GREAT ADVENTURE! BUT NOW THAT I'M REUNITED WITH MY *SHIP,* IT'S TIME TO--

YOU'RE GOING *NOWHERE,* SOLO!

Rebel headquarters on Hoth...

DON'T GET *UNDERFOOT,* YOU ROLLING BOOBY TRAP! PRINCESS LEIA MUST *HEAR* OF THIS DISASTER AT ONCE!

DIITTA-BUH VROOOP!

SCANNERS INDICATE THAT UNIDENTIFIED SHIP IS *LEAVING* THIS SYSTEM AT LAST!

THEN HAN AND LUKE WERE *SUCCESSFUL* KEEPING THIS BASE *SECRET!* WHAT'S THE *DISASTER,* THREEPIO?

YOUR HIGHNESS... MASTER LUKE, CAPTAIN SOLO, AND CHEWBACCA ARE APPARENTLY STILL *ON BOARD!*

WE WANTED THAT SHIP *GONE* BEFORE THIS NEW BASE WAS *DISCOVERED,* THREEPIO... I DIDN'T DREAM THAT WOULD REQUIRE HAN AND LUKE GOING *WITH* IT!

"WHAT HAVE THEY AND CHEWBACCA GOTTEN INTO *NOW?*"

In the hold of Raskar's ship... a *SURPRISE* awaits the returning heroes!

WE BOARDED AND TOOK CONTROL WHILE YOU WERE PLAYIN' *GAMES* ON THAT *ICE PLANET,* PIRATE!

WE'RE *BOUNTY HUNTERS...* HERE TO RELIEVE YOU OF *CAPTAIN SOLO!*

HAN, MY FRIEND... THESE ARE *NOT* MEMBERS OF MY CREW!

BOUNTY HUNTERS! ON *MY* SHIP! IF I WEREN'T INJURED--

BUT YOU *ARE,* RASKAR... SO SPARE US ANY THREATS! YOU MIGHT *SURVIVE* THIS...

IT'S *HAN SOLO* AN' HIS PALS WHO INTEREST US! YOU'LL GET YOUR SHIP BACK AT OUR *DESTINATION!*

YOU'RE TAKING US TO *JABBA THE HUTT?!*

THAT WILL BE DECIDED BY THE *ORGANIZER* OF THIS HUNTING EXPEDITION, SOLO... *BOBA FETT!*

OH, *NO!* YOUR HIGHNESS, THE UNKNOWN VESSEL WITH MASTER LUKE AND CAPTAIN SOLO ABOARD IS MAKING THE JUMP TO *HYPERSPACE!*

THEY'VE SUCCESSFULLY PROTECTED THIS BASE FROM *DISCOVERY*, THREEPIO...

"...BUT AT WHAT *COST* TO THEMSELVES?"

THEY'VE LOCKED *RASKAR* AWAY WITH HIS CREW, HAN, WHERE DOES THAT LEAVE *US?*

WHO KNOWS, WITH A BUNCH OF STRANGE *BOUNTY HUNTERS*, LUKE?

YOU HAVEN'T LOOKED *CLOSELY*, SOLO...WE'RE NOT *ALL* STRANGERS!

LET ME STEP INTO THE *LIGHT*, SOLO...YOU'LL SEE THERE'S *ONE* BOUNTY HUNTER HERE THAT YOU *KNOW!*

ONE YOU *ALMOST* DESTROYED!

SKORR! YOU TRIED NAILING US ON ORD MANTELL!

AND *YOU* TRICKED ME INTO THE *IMPERIALS'* HANDS! I WAS SENTENCED TO THE *SPICE MINES OF KESSEL!*

THESE *OTHERS* THREW IN WITH BOBA FETT FOR *REWARD,* SOLO... I'M IN FOR *REVENGE!*

I *SUFFERED* IN THE SPICE MINES OF KESSEL BECAUSE OF YOU, HAN SOLO... AND I WON'T REST UNTIL YOU *PAY* FOR IT!

SKORR!

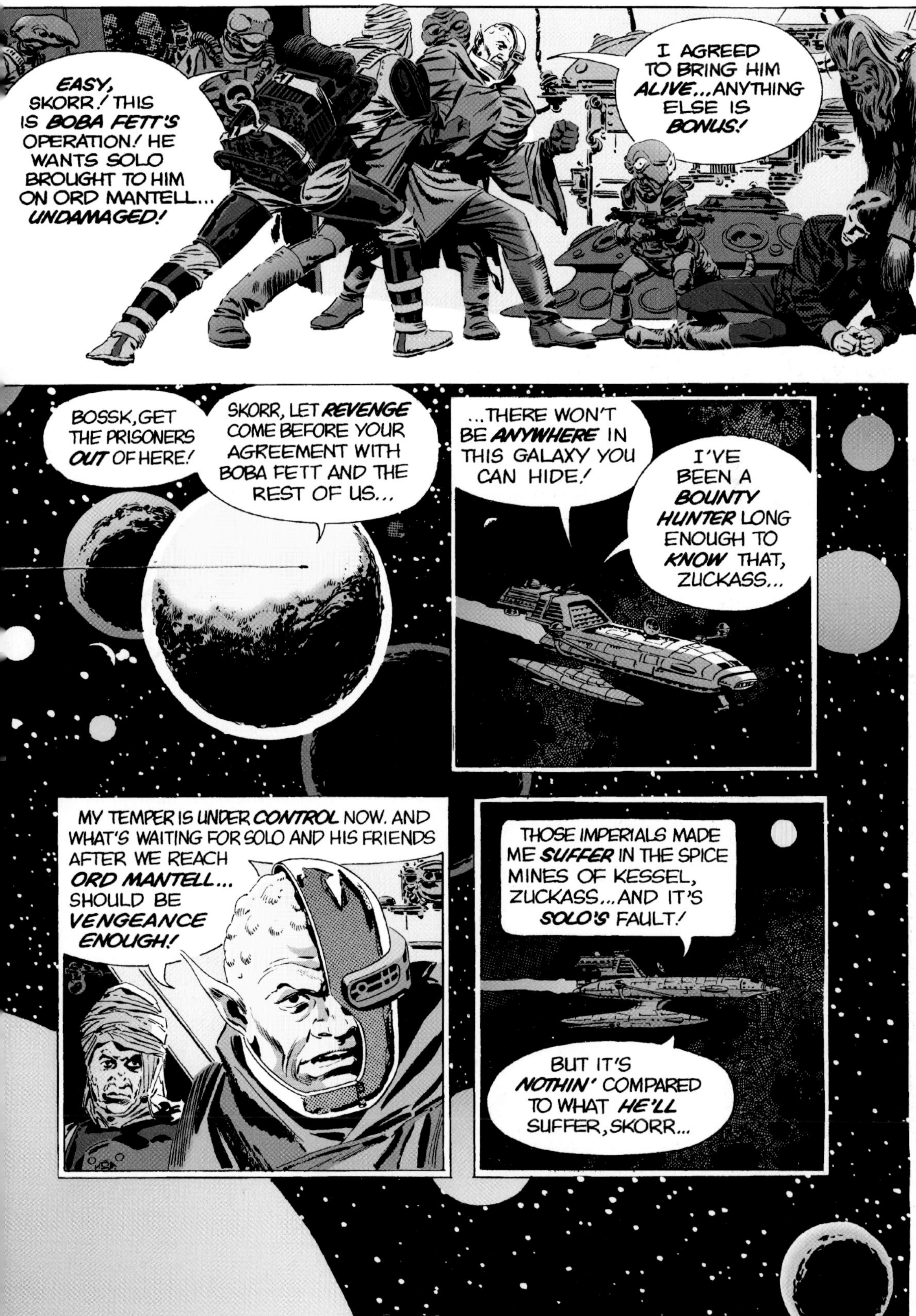
EASY, SKORR! THIS IS BOBA FETT'S OPERATION! HE WANTS SOLO BROUGHT TO HIM ON ORD MANTELL... UNDAMAGED!
I AGREED TO BRING HIM ALIVE... ANYTHING ELSE IS BONUS!
BOSSK, GET THE PRISONERS OUT OF HERE!
SKORR, LET REVENGE COME BEFORE YOUR AGREEMENT WITH BOBA FETT AND THE REST OF US...
...THERE WON'T BE ANYWHERE IN THIS GALAXY YOU CAN HIDE!
I'VE BEEN A BOUNTY HUNTER LONG ENOUGH TO KNOW THAT, ZUCKASS...
MY TEMPER IS UNDER CONTROL NOW. AND WHAT'S WAITING FOR SOLO AND HIS FRIENDS AFTER WE REACH ORD MANTELL... SHOULD BE VENGEANCE ENOUGH!
THOSE IMPERIALS MADE ME SUFFER IN THE SPICE MINES OF KESSEL, ZUCKASS... AND IT'S SOLO'S FAULT!
BUT IT'S NOTHIN' COMPARED TO WHAT HE'LL SUFFER, SKORR...

WHEN BOBA FETT ULTIMATELY HANDS HIM OVER TO *JABBA THE HUTT!*

YES! *THAT* HAPPY THOUGHT IS ALL THAT KEEPS ME FROM KILLING HIM MYSELF!

While in one of the huge pirate vessel's cargo holds...

HAN, WHAT ARE WE GOING TO *DO?*

UH,...I WAS KIND'A HOPIN' *YOU* HAD A PLAN, LUKE!

NOT STRUNG UP LIKE *THIS!* AT LEAST WE'VE GOT UNTIL WE REACH *ORD MANTELL...*

FROM THE *DEATH STAR* ON, YOU'VE ALWAYS BEEN GOOD WITH *PLANS,* KID. CAN'T YOU THINK OF *SOMETHING?*

BAD NEWS, LUKE! THAT *SOUND* IS THE SUB-SPACE ENGINES KICKIN' BACK IN...WE'VE *REACHED* ORD MANTELL!

As the captured pirate ship draws nearer its destination...

LOOK AT *THAT!* SEEMS WE'RE NOT THE *ONLY* ONES VISITING ORD MANTELL!

SOMEONE FROM THE *EMPIRE'S* HERE!

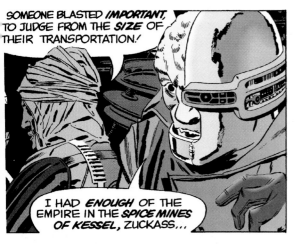

SOMEONE BLASTED *IMPORTANT*, TO JUDGE FROM THE *SIZE* OF THEIR TRANSPORTATION!

I HAD *ENOUGH* OF THE EMPIRE IN THE *SPICE MINES* OF *KESSEL*, ZUCKASS...

...AND *HAN SOLO* HELPED PUT ME THERE! I DON'T WANT IMPERIALS GRABBING *HIM*... OR *US! LET'S MOVE!*

EASY, SKORR! WE'RE NOT AMATEURS...WE WON'T GET *CAUGHT!*

On the planet...

IT IS SCARCELY *IMPERIAL POLICY* TO DEAL WITH YOUR KIND, FETT.

I THOUGHT *DARTH VADER* MADE HIS *OWN* POLICY...PARTICULARLY WHEN IT CONCERNS SOMETHING HE *WANTS!*

MY *SHUTTLE* IS TAKING ON SUPPLIES...

...YOU'VE UNTIL THAT'S *DONE* TO PROVE YOU'RE NOT WASTING MY *TIME!*

YOU SEEK CERTAIN *REBELS,* LORD VADER...

...SO DOES MY *EMPLOYER,* JABBA THE HUTT! POSSIBLY IN SATISFYING *HIM*... I CAN SATISFY *YOU* ALSO!

A *PARTICULAR* REBEL INTERESTS ME, BOBA FETT... *LUKE SKYWALKER!*

...*SOLO* COULD SERVE THAT FUNCTION *BEFORE* WE GIVE HIM TO JABBA!

A COMPANION OF THE MAN *I'M* AFTER... *HAN SOLO!*

ONE MIGHT *LURE* THE OTHER, LORD VADER! SHOULD MY FELLOW BOUNTY HUNTERS *SUCCEED*...

AND COLLECT *TWO* REWARDS INSTEAD OF *ONE,* BOUNTY HUNTER?

YOU'RE *ENTERPRISING,* FETT! PERHAPS WE WILL MEET AGAIN... WHEN YOUR ENTERPRISE BEARS *FRUIT!*

A pleased Boba Fett watches Darth Vader's departure from Ord Mantell...

...visions of a *DOUBLE* reward in his mind...

...if his bounty hunter *PARTNERS* enjoy success!

ORD MANTELL'S *BELOW,* RASKAR! WE'RE *LEAVING*...WITH SOLO AND OUR OTHER PRISONERS!

WITHOUT *FREEING* US?

MY CREW AND I ARE STILL *LOCKED* IN THIS CARGO HOLD!

WE SAID WE'D LET YOU *SURVIVE,* PIRATE... WE DIDN'T PROMISE YOU'D *ENJOY* THE CIRCUMSTANCES!

"YOU RASCAL, SKORR!"

WE DON'T *NEED* THEM, SOLO! THE SHIP'S SET ON *AUTO-CONTROL!*

THEY'LL DRIFT *FOREVER* IN DEEP SPACE!

DON'T *WORRY,* CORELLIAN! WHEN WE MEET WITH *BOBA FETT* AND TURN YOU OVER TO *JABBA*... YOU, SKYWALKER, AND THE WOOKIEE WON'T GET OFF *NEARLY* SO EASILY!

Bounty hunters and prisoners land in Ord Mantell's back country...

AN ABANDONED *MOISTURE PLANT?*

WHERE GREEDY COMPETITORS CAN'T *SPOT* YOU, SOLO! BUT... WHERE'S *BOBA FETT?*

THERE'S A *MESSAGE* FROM HIM, SKORR! HE'S AT THE MAIN SPACEPORT...TO MEET WITH *DARTH VADER!*

WHAT?!

HAN! IF BOBA FETT'S TEAMED WITH *DARTH VADER,* THAT MEANS--

HE'S FOUND SOMETHING *WORSE* THAN DELIVERING US TO *JABBA THE HUTT!*

AND IT LOOKS LIKE OUR OLD BUDDY, *SKORR,* IS JUST ABOUT AS *THRILLED* BY THE NEWS AS *WE* ARE! THINGS ARE *ONLY* GONNA GET *ROUGHER* FOR US!

WHY IS BOBA FETT DEALING WITH THE *EMPIRE?* I HAD *ENOUGH* OF THEM IN THE SPICE MINES OF KESSEL!

BUT YOU *ESCAPED,* SKORR...

...WHY FUSS NOW IF IT MEANS MORE *PROFIT* FOR US ALL?

SEE THE *PRISONERS* ARE SECURE AND QUIT *COMPLAINING!*

SKORR'S COMING IN TO *CHECK* ON US, HAN,... TRY TO GET HIM *ANGRY!*

ANGRY? LUKE, HE *HATES* ME! HE'LL LEAP AT *ANY* EXCUSE...

...TO POUND ME INTO *OOZE* WHILE WE'RE CHAINED UP LIKE THIS!

WELL... AT LEAST I'M NOT ASKING THE *IMPOSSIBLE!*

Departing Ord Mantell, Darth Vader communicates with...the *EMPEROR!*

THIS DAY, MY MASTER, THE FLEET BEGINS ITS SEARCH FOR THE NEW *REBEL BASE!*

YET YOU MAKE *OTHER* ARRANGEMENTS ALSO?

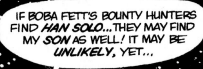

IF BOBA FETT'S BOUNTY HUNTERS FIND *HAN SOLO*...THEY MAY FIND MY *SON* AS WELL! IT MAY BE *UNLIKELY,* YET...

SOMETIMES THE *REMOTE* PATH LEADS TO THE GOAL FIRST. YOU *PLEASE* ME, MY SERVANT!

Skorr enters...glowering at the trio of prisoners!

GOOD! JUST AS I NOTICED *EARLIER!* NOW, IF *HAN* COMES THROUGH!

PITIFUL, ISN'T IT, CHEWIE? SKORR WAS A SHARP *OPPONENT* LAST TIME WE CLASHED...NOW HE'S A *FLUNKY* FOR BOBA FETT AND HIS OTHER *BOUNTY HUNTERS!*

GUESS ALL THAT TIME IN THE SPICE MINES OF KESSEL *BROKE* HIM! TURNED HIM INTO--

SOLO! YOU'LL PAY!

Han's goading words bring Skorr violently charging!

BOWWRRRRRAAARRRK!

SOLO'S WOOKIEE *PARTNER!* WHY SHOULD HE SUDDENLY *HOWL* SO?!

LET'S FIND OUT *FAST!* WE DON'T WANT *BOBA FETT* RETURNIN' TO FIND *DAMAGED* MERCHANDISE!

Before Skorr's attack can go further...

WE **WARNED** YOU ABOUT LETTING THIS GET **PERSONAL!**

SOLO **PROVOKED** ME! JUST KEEP ME **AWAY** FROM HIM!

The bounty hunters hustle their furious associate outside...

MAYBE I'M STILL PUNCHY...BUT...WHAT DID THAT **ACCOMPLISH,** LUKE?

PLENTY, HAN!

HE WAS **CLOSE** ENOUGH THAT EVEN A NOVICE AT THE **FORCE** LIKE YOURS TRULY...COULD GET THE **LIGHTSABER** FROM HIS BELT TO MY **HAND!**

SKORR'S BEEN CARRYING MY **LIGHTSABER** WITH HIM SINCE WE WERE FIRST **DISARMED...** HE'S **NOT** ANYMORE!

NOW... LET'S SEE IF I CAN CUT US ALL **FREE!**

BEING **FREE** IS WORTH A BEATING FROM SKORR!

THE **DISTRACTION** ENABLED ME TO USE THE **FORCE** TO LIFT MY **LIGHTSABER** FROM HIS BELT...

...BUT EVEN AFTER I SLICE A WAY **OUT,** WE'VE **STILL** GOT TROUBLE!

His lightsaber regained...Luke frees himself, Han, and Chewie! Then...

I'VE CUT THROUGH THE *REAR WALL!*

GREAT, KID! WHILE OUR BOUNTY-HUNTING HOSTS ARE YAKKIN' OUT *FRONT*...WE'LL BE LONG GONE OUT *BACK!*

THEY'RE TALKIN' ON A *COMLINK!* I WONDER WHO --?

A ship streaks low over the Ord Mantell wastelands... Boba Fett's *SLAVE I!*

ZUCKASS! YOUR GROUP'S *BACK?* WHAT *NEWS?!*

THE *BEST!* WE NOT ONLY FOLLOWED YOUR LEAD TO *SOLO...*

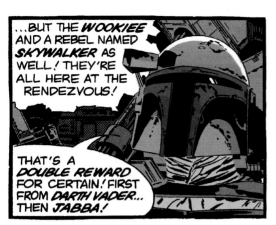

...BUT THE *WOOKIEE* AND A REBEL NAMED *SKYWALKER* AS WELL! THEY'RE ALL HERE AT THE RENDEZVOUS!

THAT'S A *DOUBLE REWARD* FOR CERTAIN! FIRST FROM *DARTH VADER*... THEN *JABBA!*

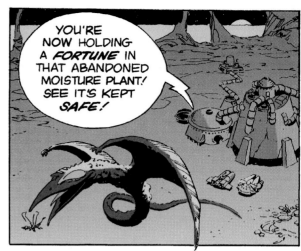

YOU'RE NOW HOLDING A *FORTUNE* IN THAT ABANDONED MOISTURE PLANT! SEE IT'S KEPT *SAFE!*

...WE JUST BROKE UP A *FIGHT!* NOTHING SERIOUS THOUGH...

Boba Fett's *SLAVE I* lands at the bounty hunters' lair...

FOOLS! WHILE YOU WERE ON THE COM-LINK WITH *ME*... YOUR PRISONERS WERE *ESCAPING!*

I SAW THEM RUNNING OUT THE *REAR* OF THE MOISTURE PLANT AS I FLEW OVER!

AFTER THEM!

THEY HEADED INTO THE *DESERT*...WITHOUT TIME TO DISGUISE THEIR *TRACKS!*

WE'LL *NAIL* 'EM BEFORE THEY GET *FAR!*

The bounty hunters, led by Boba Fett, follow the tracks away from the moisture plant...

IT'S *WORKIN'*, LUKE!

ONLY UNTIL THEY GET BEYOND THAT *RISE*, HAN...

...AND FIND THE TRAIL SUDDENLY *ENDS!* WALKING *BACKWARDS* IN YOUR OWN TRACKS IS A TRICK THE *SAND PEOPLE* USE ON TATOOINE, BUT--

IT'S *GOOD* ENOUGH, KID! ALL WE NEED IS TIME TO REACH THE *FALCON*... AND *BLAST OFF!*

The three Star Warriors rush for the *MILLENNIUM FALCON* and escape!

THOSE BOUNTY HUNTERS WILL DISCOVER OUR TRACKS ARE *FALSE* ANY MOMENT NOW, HAN!

WE'LL BE ROCKETIN' *AWAY* WHILE THEY'RE STILL RUNNIN' *BACK* HERE!

DON'T *BET* ON IT, SOLO!

SKORR! YOU DIDN'T RUSH OFF WITH *BOBA FETT* AN' THE OTHERS!

I HUNG *BACK*, SOLO...KNOWING YOU WOULDN'T GO *FAR* FROM YOUR SHIP!

IN FACT, I WAS PURPOSELY *CARELESS* WITH YOUNG SKYWALKER'S *LIGHTSABER* SO YOU *COULD* ESCAPE!

BUT... *WHY*?

I HATE THE *EMPIRE* NEARLY AS MUCH AS I HATE *YOU*! BEFORE LETTING BOBA FETT TURN YOU OVER TO *DARTH VADER*...I'D RATHER *KILL* YOU!

SKORR, IF YOU BLAST ME... YOU'LL GET MUCH *LESS* BOUNTY FROM JABBA!

WE'D NEVER *REACH* THE HUTT, SOLO... NOT WITH *BOBA FETT* ON OUR TRAIL!

MY *BEST* REVENGE AGAINST YOU--AND THE *EMPIRE*--FOR MY TIME IN THEIR SPICE MINES ON KESSEL...

...IS TO *KILL* YOU AND YOUR FRIENDS *RIGHT NOW*!

AT LEAST MAKE IT A *FAIR* FIGHT!

THROW YOU A *BLASTER*? THERE ISN'T *TIME* TO BE SPORTING, SOLO!

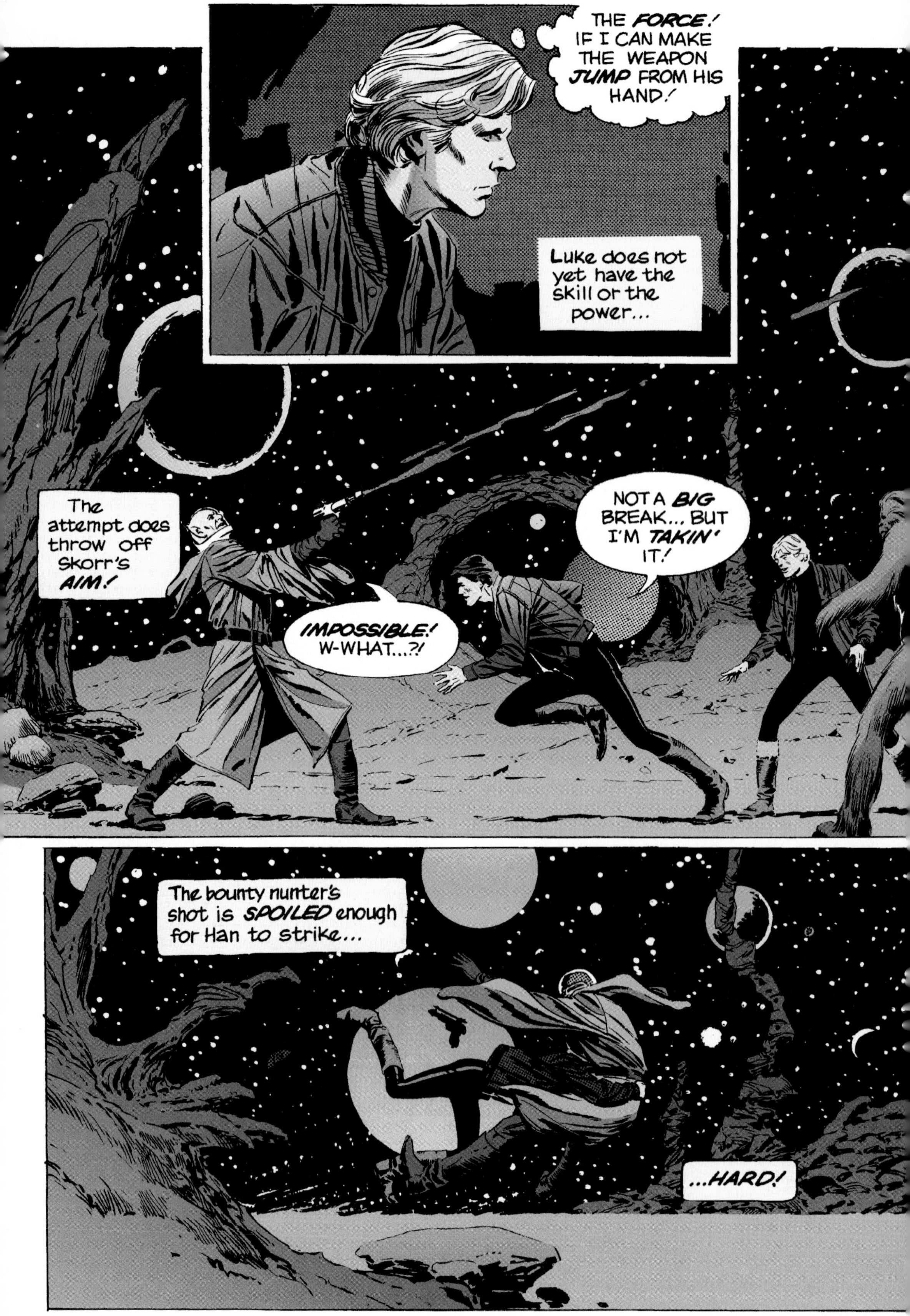
THE FORCE! IF I CAN MAKE THE WEAPON JUMP FROM HIS HAND!
Luke does not yet have the skill or the power...
The attempt does throw off Skorr's AIM!
IMPOSSIBLE! W-WHAT...?!
NOT A BIG BREAK... BUT I'M TAKIN' IT!
The bounty hunter's shot is SPOILED enough for Han to strike...
...HARD!

Before Luke and Chewbacca can reach them, Han and Skorr grapple for the blaster! Then...

N-NO!

HE WAS SO *ANXIOUS* TO KILL ME... HE TRIGGERED THE GUN WHILE I WAS STILL SHOVIN' THE BARREL *HIS* WAY!

SKORR'S NOT OUR *ONLY* WORRY, HAN!

VARROWWWRRRLL!

YEAH, CHEWIE... *BOBA FETT* AND HIS *BOUNTY HUNTERS!* LUKE WAS *RIGHT*...THEY DIDN'T STAY TRICKED *LONG!*

AND THEY'LL BE *ALL OVER* US BEFORE WE CAN GET THE *FALCON* ALOFT!

Suddenly...

THE *MOISTURE PLANT!* WHAT *HIT* IT?!

HAN! IT'S *RASKAR'S* PIRATE SHIP. BY THE TIME BOBA FETT AND HIS BOUNTY HUNTERS RECOVER FROM *THIS* ATTACK... WE'LL BE SAFE ON *HOTH!*

And...

HEY, YOU BEARDED SURPRISE PARTY! THE LAST *I* RECALL... YOU WERE LOCKED IN YOUR OWN HOLD AN' HEADED BY AUTO-CONTROL FOR *DEEP SPACE!*

Above the surface of Ord Mantell... two ships part!

SOLO, MY FRIEND... IT'S DIFFICULT TO BECOME A *PIRATE* WITHOUT FIRST BEING A *THIEF!* AND WHAT *WORTHWHILE* THIEF... IS EVER CAUGHT WITHOUT A *LOCKPICK?*

FAREWELL! I'M OFF FOR THE RIMWORLDS... AND *SAFETY!*

SINCE YOU TOOK OUT *SKORR* AFTER HE MISSED HIS SHOT AT YOU, HAN... I'D SAY OUR TROUBLES ARE *OVER!*

THE IMPERIALS MIGHT NOT *AGREE,* LUKE...

"...BUT I'M BETTIN' EVEN *THEY* CAN'T PREVENT US FROM REACHIN' OUR HOTH BASE *NOW!*"

NOTHING FROM THE *BOUNTY HUNTERS,* MY SERVANT?

I HAVE OTHER PLANS, MASTER...

THE REBELS ARE ADEPT AT *HIDING,* MY SERVANT. WITH OUR FLEETS ON THE MOVE...

...IT IS UNLIKELY *ANYTHING* CAN LURE THEM FORTH!

BUT NOT *ALL* THEIR FORCES ARE SAFE, MASTER! SOME STILL SCURRY FOR COVER! *THEY* CAN BE THE KEY TO *FINDING* THE OTHERS...

"...EVEN IF IT IS ONLY *ONE* SMALL SHIP!"

WE SEEM TO HAVE HIT A *QUIET* SECTOR OF SPACE, LUKE! SHOULD BE SAFE TO GET OFF A CODED *MESSAGE!*

BUT DON'T GET *GABBY!* THE EMPIRE *STILL* MIGHT HAVE TIME TO *TRACE* US!

HAN, I JUST WANT TO ALERT *HOTH* THAT WE'RE SAFE AND COMING HOME AND--

OH, NO!

LUKE, DON'T TELL ME THERE'S *TROUBLE!* WE'VE BEEN THROUGH *ENOUGH* TROUBLE!

BEFORE I COULD CONTACT HOTH BASE, I *PICKED UP* SOMETHING...

A REBEL *DISTRESS BEACON!*

I TOLD YOU *NOT* TO TELL ME! IT'S *GOTTA* BE A TRICK OR A TRAP!

BUT, *HAN*... WHAT IF IT *ISN'T?!*

WE'RE *NEVER* GONNA GET BACK TO HOTH AT THE RATE WE'RE GOIN', LUKE!

HAN, JUST LET ME *CHECK* WITH THEM ABOUT THAT *DISTRESS BEACON*...

...IF NO ONE IN THE REBEL COMMAND IS *UNACCOUNTED FOR*, THEN IT'S PROBABLY AN *IMPERIAL TRICK!*

I GOT A *BAD FEELIN'* ABOUT THIS...!

And...

LUKE...IT'S *WONDERFUL* TO KNOW YOU, HAN AND CHEWBACCA ARE SAFE! BUT...THIS *SITUATION!* SOMEONE *IS* MISSING!

I CAN'T *ORDER* YOU TO INVESTIGATE THE REBEL DISTRESS BEACON YOU'VE PICKED UP, LUKE...

...BUT I'M AFRAID YOU'LL *INSIST* UPON IT!

THEN, TALK TO *ME* INSTEAD, YOUR ROYALNESS...HAN SOLO *NEVER* PLAYS HERO IF HE DOESN'T *HAVE* TO!

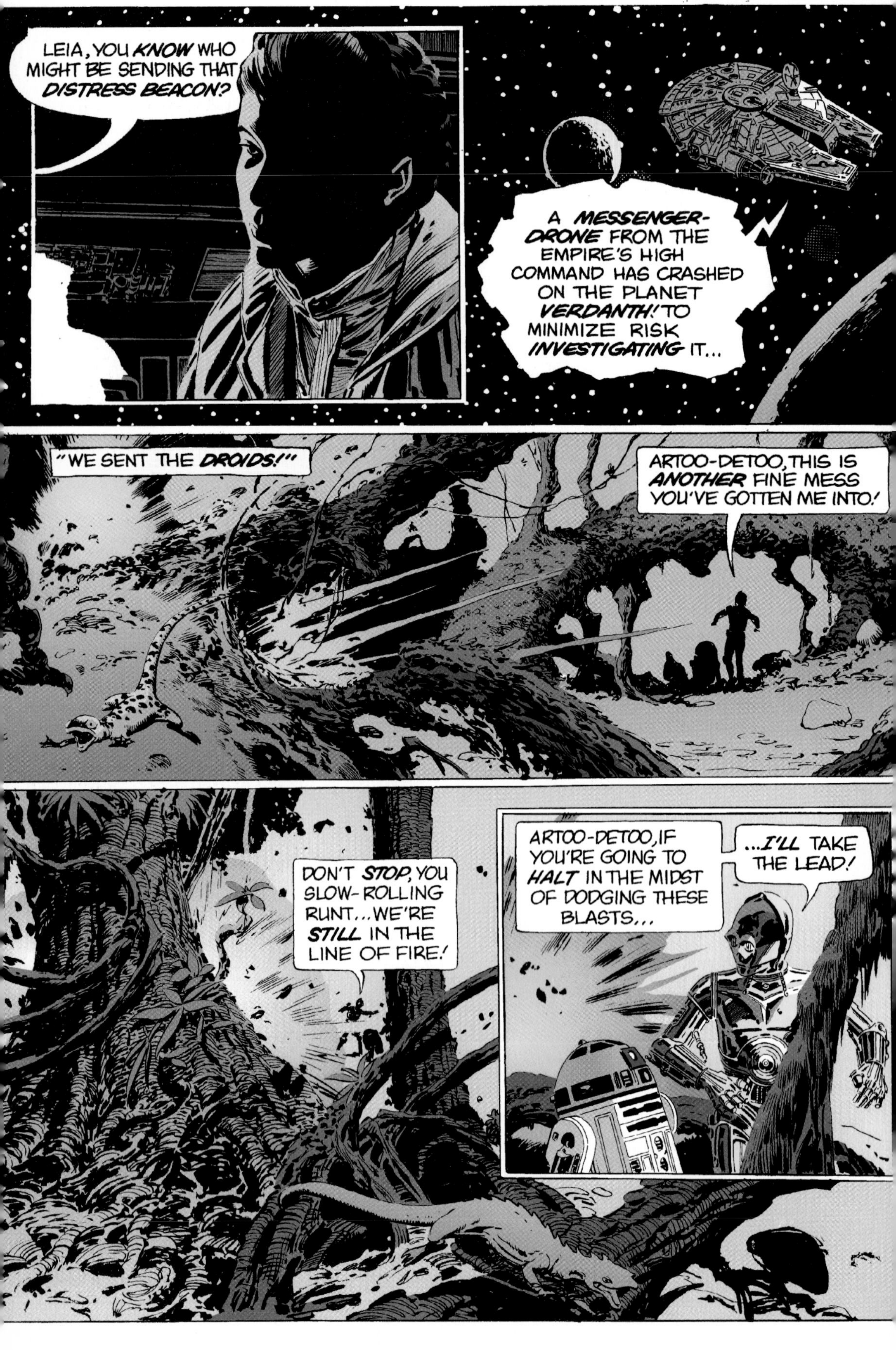
LEIA, YOU KNOW WHO MIGHT BE SENDING THAT DISTRESS BEACON?
A MESSENGER-DRONE FROM THE EMPIRE'S HIGH COMMAND HAS CRASHED ON THE PLANET VERDANTH! TO MINIMIZE RISK INVESTIGATING IT...
"WE SENT THE DROIDS!"
ARTOO-DETOO, THIS IS ANOTHER FINE MESS YOU'VE GOTTEN ME INTO!
DON'T STOP, YOU SLOW-ROLLING RUNT...WE'RE STILL IN THE LINE OF FIRE!
ARTOO-DETOO, IF YOU'RE GOING TO HALT IN THE MIDST OF DODGING THESE BLASTS...
...I'LL TAKE THE LEAD!

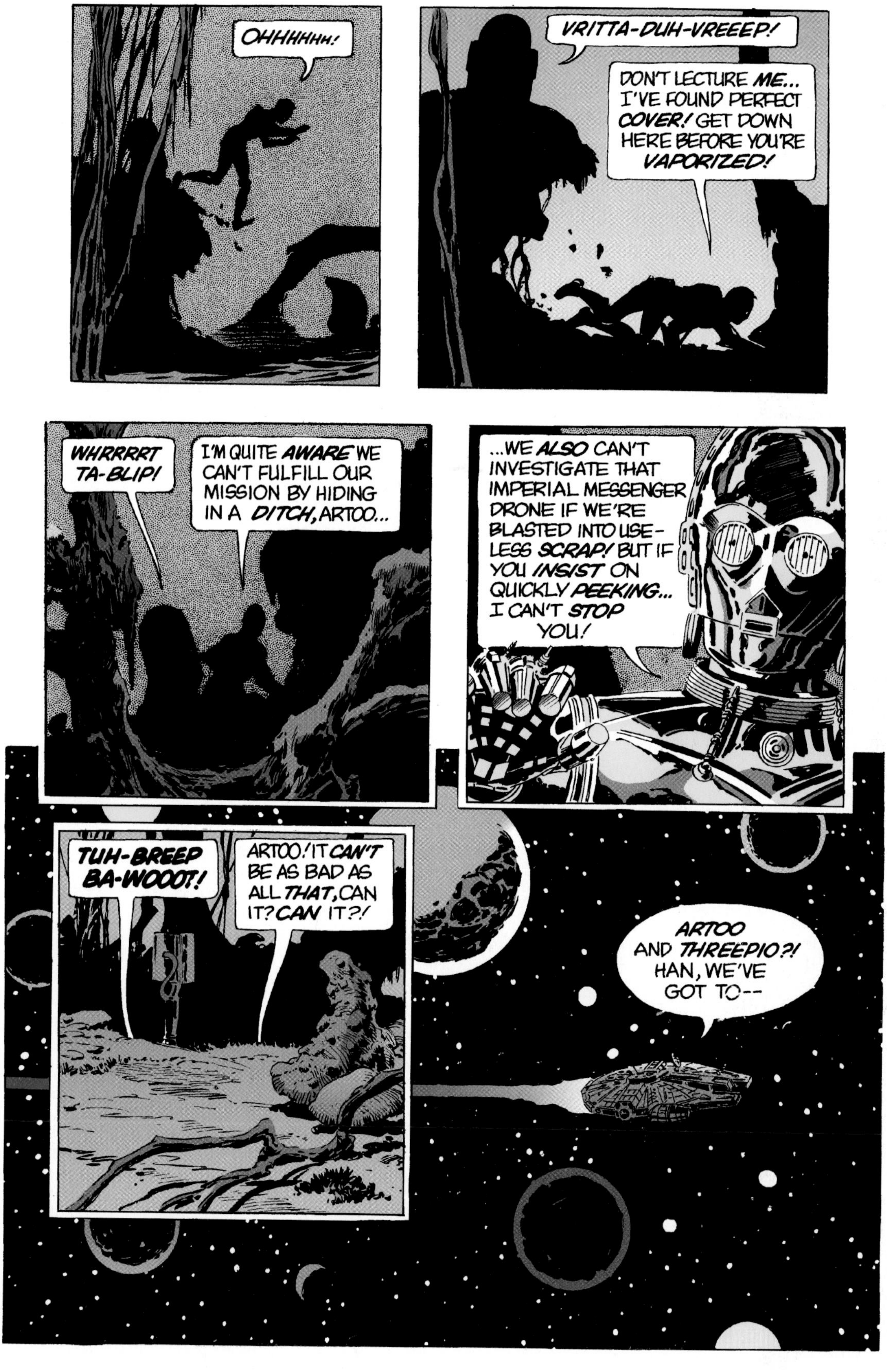
OHHHHHH!
VRITTA-DUH-VREEEP!
DON'T LECTURE ME... I'VE FOUND PERFECT COVER! GET DOWN HERE BEFORE YOU'RE VAPORIZED!
WHRRRRT TA-BLIP!
I'M QUITE AWARE WE CAN'T FULFILL OUR MISSION BY HIDING IN A DITCH, ARTOO...
...WE ALSO CAN'T INVESTIGATE THAT IMPERIAL MESSENGER DRONE IF WE'RE BLASTED INTO USE-LESS SCRAP! BUT IF YOU INSIST ON QUICKLY PEEKING... I CAN'T STOP YOU!
TUH-BREEP BA-WOOOT!
ARTOO! IT CAN'T BE AS BAD AS ALL THAT, CAN IT? CAN IT?!
ARTOO AND THREEPIO?! HAN, WE'VE GOT TO--

I KNOW, I KNOW! WE'VE GOTTA *RESCUE* THEM! IT'S NOT LIKE WE'VE *DONE* MUCH LATELY...EXCEPT DECOY *PIRATES* AND DUEL *BOUNTY HUNTERS!* BESIDES...

YOU'RE *RIGHT*, ARTOO! THERE'S NO *END* TO THE EMPIRE'S CRUELTY...CREATING A MESSENGER DRONE THAT WILL *ATTACK* ITS OWN KIND...

...PARTICULARLY WHEN THAT KIND IS *US!*

"...HOW MUCH TROUBLE CAN TWO *DROIDS* BE IN?"

Meanwhile...

CAPTAIN, THE SPECIAL LASERWAVE TRANSMISSION! LORD VADER'S *TRAP* HAS ATTRACTED SOMEONE!

HE'LL WISH TO KNOW *IMMEDIATELY!*

WAIT! ACCORDING TO THIS *INFORMATION* YOU'RE RECEIVING, LORD VADER'S TRAP HAS BEEN SPRUNG BY... *DROIDS.?!*

DISAPPOINTING SIR! BUT...PERHAPS *SOMETHING* WILL COME OF IT!

And...

HAN, YOU'RE GOING TO HELP RESCUE ARTOO AND THREEPIO WITHOUT EVEN *GRIPING?*

I DON'T BELIEVE I'M *DOING* THIS! AFTER ALL WE'VE *ALREADY* BEEN THROUGH, I'M PLAYIN' HERO *AGAIN*...

...AND FOR TWO *DROIDS!* NO SELF-RESPECTING *SCOUNDREL* DOES THAT!

COME *ON,* HAN! ARTOO AND THREEPIO HAVE BEEN THROUGH *PLENTY* FOR US! HOW COULD WE *NOT* RESCUE THEM?!

I DON'T KNOW, LUKE... WE'RE DROPPIN' OUT OF *HYPERSPACE,* CHEWIE! WHAT KIND OF *READIN'* CAN YOU GIVE ON OUR DESTINATION?

WAURRGHHH!

IT'S A *JUNGLE PLANET?* I *HATE* JUNGLE PLANETS! ALL THAT *FOLIAGE...* CAN'T SEE WHAT'S *SNEAKIN' UP* ON YOU!

YOUR DROIDS BETTER *APPRECIATE* THIS, LUKE!

FIREWORKS *ALREADY!* WHEN YOUR DROIDS GET INTO TROUBLE, LUKE...THEY DON'T FOOL AROUND!

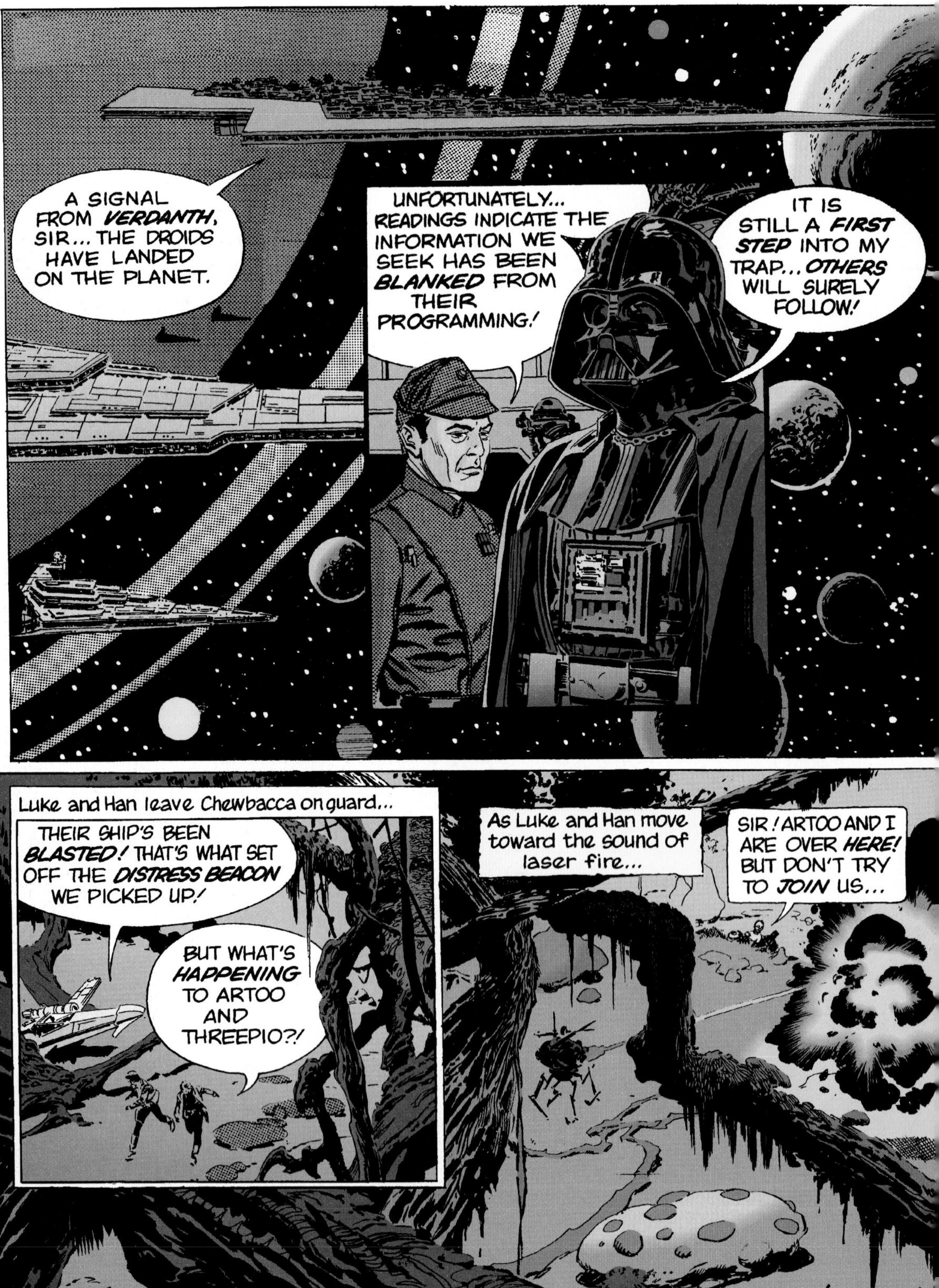
A SIGNAL FROM VERDANTH, SIR... THE DROIDS HAVE LANDED ON THE PLANET.
UNFORTUNATELY... READINGS INDICATE THE INFORMATION WE SEEK HAS BEEN BLANKED FROM THEIR PROGRAMMING!
IT IS STILL A FIRST STEP INTO MY TRAP... OTHERS WILL SURELY FOLLOW!
Luke and Han leave Chewbacca on guard...
THEIR SHIP'S BEEN BLASTED! THAT'S WHAT SET OFF THE DISTRESS BEACON WE PICKED UP!
BUT WHAT'S HAPPENING TO ARTOO AND THREEPIO?!
As Luke and Han move toward the sound of laser fire...
SIR! ARTOO AND I ARE OVER HERE! BUT DON'T TRY TO JOIN US...

...THAT IMPERIAL MESSENGER DRONE IS BLASTING ANYTHING THAT *MOVES!*

WE'VE GOT *NO CHOICE,* GOLDENROD! YOU'RE OCCUPYING THE *ONLY* SAFE COVER AROUND!

I'M *SORRY,* MASTER LUKE! THAT MECHANIZED MONSTROSITY OF THE EMPIRE SEEMS *DETERMINED* TO VAPORIZE ME AND ARTOO-DETOO...

...NOW IT'S BOUND TO GET *YOU* AND *CAPTAIN SOLO* AS WELL!

MAYBE, THREEPIO! BUT, FUNNY... IT SEEMS TO HAVE *STOPPED* FIRING!

LORD VADER! NEW TRANSMISSION FROM THE DRONE ON VERDANTH... IT NOW HAS *HUMAN* CONTACT!

Excitement sweeps Darth Vader's battle cruiser...

HUMAN REBELS ARE NEAR THE MESSENGER DRONE? QUICKLY, THEN! TO THE *CYBERNETIC CHAMBER...*

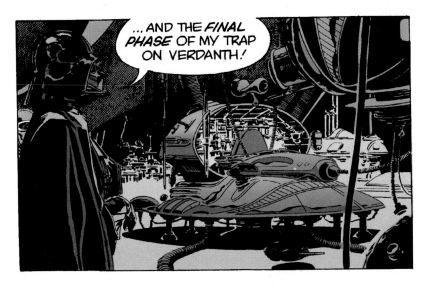

...AND THE *FINAL PHASE* OF MY TRAP ON VERDANTH!

On Verdanth...

WHAT DO YOU THINK'S GOIN' ON WITH THAT THING LUKE?

TIME TO *INVESTIGATE!*

COULD THAT MESSENGER DRONE BE PROGRAMMED TO SHOOT ONLY AT *DROIDS?*

IT SURE *STOPPED* ONCE WE ARRIVED, HAN! EVEN IF IT'S RIGGED TO *ALERT* THE EMPIRE...

...THERE ARE NO *IMPERIAL SHIPS* IN VERDANTH'S VICINITY! *NOTHING* TO STOP US FROM GRABBING ITS INFORMATION THAT I CAN SEE!

But aboard Darth Vader's cruiser...

CYBERNETIC CIRCUITRY READY TO CONNECT!

SOON I'LL DEAL *DIRECTLY* WITH WHICHEVER HAPLESS REBEL HAS SPRUNG OUR *TRAP* ON VERDANTH!

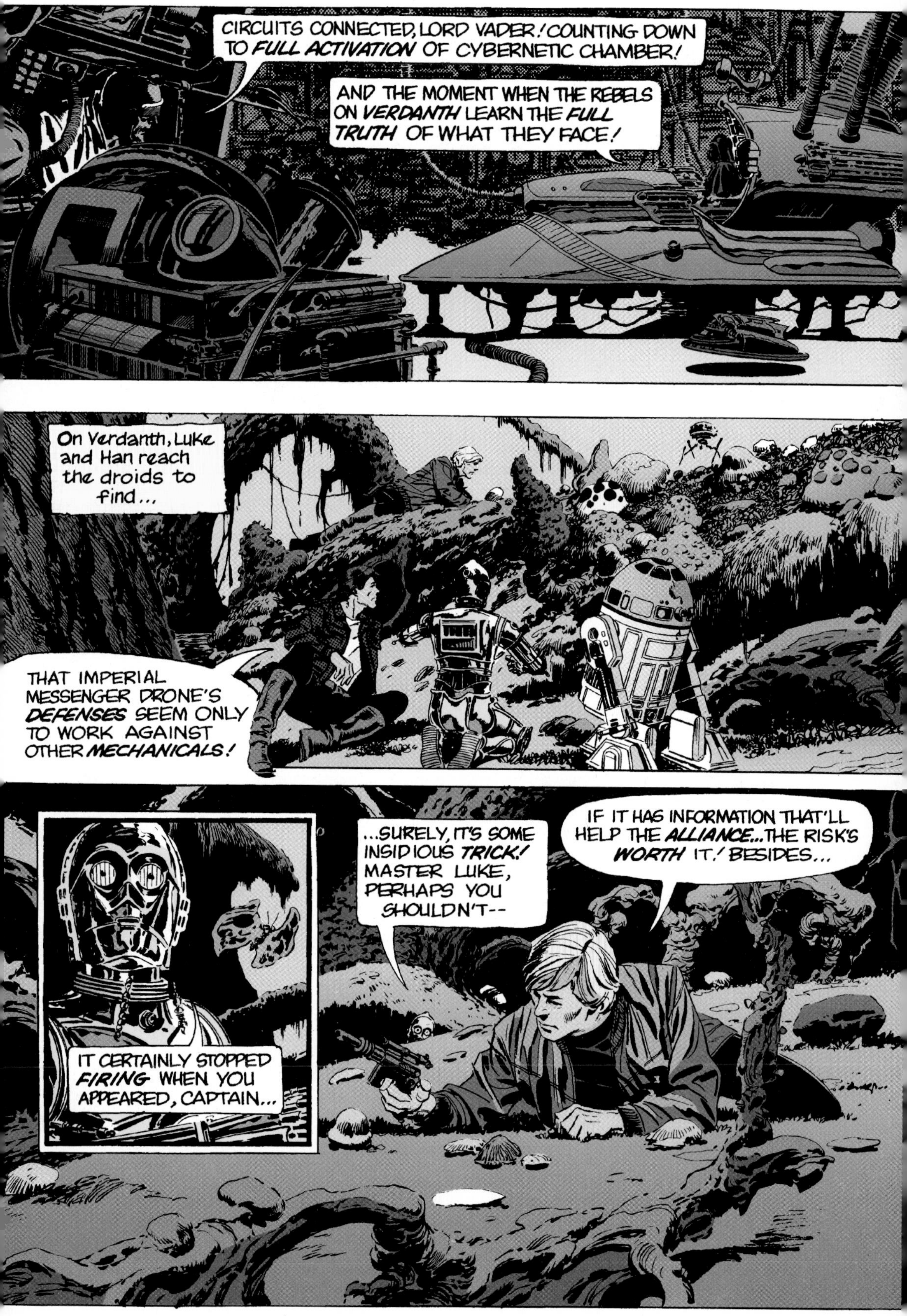
CIRCUITS CONNECTED, LORD VADER! COUNTING DOWN TO FULL ACTIVATION OF CYBERNETIC CHAMBER!
AND THE MOMENT WHEN THE REBELS ON VERDANTH LEARN THE FULL TRUTH OF WHAT THEY FACE!
On Verdanth, Luke and Han reach the droids to find...
THAT IMPERIAL MESSENGER DRONE'S DEFENSES SEEM ONLY TO WORK AGAINST OTHER MECHANICALS!
IT CERTAINLY STOPPED FIRING WHEN YOU APPEARED, CAPTAIN...
...SURELY, IT'S SOME INSIDIOUS TRICK! MASTER LUKE, PERHAPS YOU SHOULDN'T--
IF IT HAS INFORMATION THAT'LL HELP THE ALLIANCE...THE RISK'S WORTH IT! BESIDES...

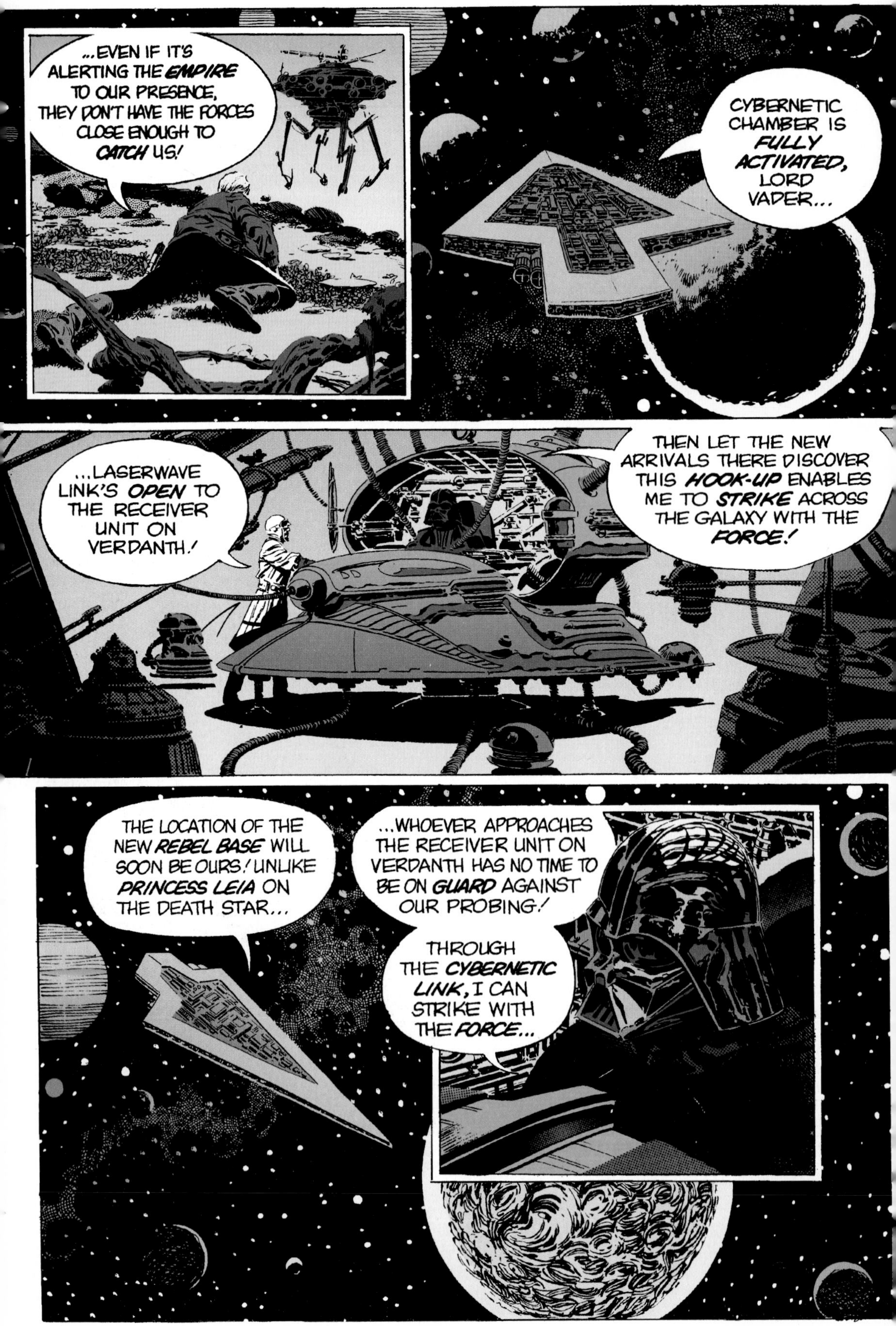
...EVEN IF IT'S ALERTING THE EMPIRE TO OUR PRESENCE, THEY DON'T HAVE THE FORCES CLOSE ENOUGH TO CATCH US!
CYBERNETIC CHAMBER IS FULLY ACTIVATED, LORD VADER...
...LASERWAVE LINK'S OPEN TO THE RECEIVER UNIT ON VERDANTH!
THEN LET THE NEW ARRIVALS THERE DISCOVER THIS HOOK-UP ENABLES ME TO STRIKE ACROSS THE GALAXY WITH THE FORCE!
THE LOCATION OF THE NEW REBEL BASE WILL SOON BE OURS! UNLIKE PRINCESS LEIA ON THE DEATH STAR...
...WHOEVER APPROACHES THE RECEIVER UNIT ON VERDANTH HAS NO TIME TO BE ON GUARD AGAINST OUR PROBING!
THROUGH THE CYBERNETIC LINK, I CAN STRIKE WITH THE FORCE...

"...AND WREST THE INFORMATION FROM HIS *MIND!* JUST A FEW MORE *STEPS* WILL DO IT."

MASTER LUKE! I WISH YOU WOULDN'T *DO* THIS, SIR!

YEAH, KID! GOLDENROD'S BEGINNIN' TO MAKE *ME* NERVOUS ABOUT YOU! C'MON BACK!

IN A *MOMENT!* I'M OPENING THE MESSENGER DRONE'S *INFORMATION STORAGE MODULE* NOW SO--

SILENCE! THIS ISN'T ANY *ORDINARY* REBEL WHOSE MIND I COULD EASILY PROBE...

WE'VE *FULL* CYBERNETIC CONTACT WITH OUR PREY, LORD VADER! HAVE YOU REACHED HIM WITH THE *FORCE?*

"IT'S YOUNG *SKYWALKER!* BUT WHATEVER THERE IS OF THE FORCE *PROTECTING* HIM... HE HASN'T ENOUGH *MASTERY* TO RESIST ME *LONG!*"

LUKE! WHAT *IS* IT?! WHAT *ABOUT* THE MESSENGER DRONE AND THE *FORCE?!*

SHOOT IT, CAPTAIN SOLO! EVEN IF IT *IS* A FELLOW MECHANICAL!

As Luke attempts to retrieve information from the Imperial messenger drone...
DARTH VADER STRIKES!

NOOOOOOO!

T-THE *FORCE!* SOMEONE...REACHING OUT..., *THROUGH* THE MACHINE!

CAPTAIN SOLO, WE CAN'T JUST *ABANDON* MASTER LUKE TO HIS FATE!

I'LL KEEP *FIRIN'*, THREEPIO! MAYBE THAT IMPERIAL DRONE'S FORCE FIELD WILL *WEAKEN...*

...BUT IT'S SURE NOT SHOWIN' ANY *SIGNS* OF IT!

OH, DEAR, MASTER LUKE IS *DOOMED!*

SKYWALKER! OF ALL THE REBELS WHO *MIGHT* HAVE FALLEN INTO MY TRAP ON VERDANTH!

THE *FORCE* IS STRONG ENOUGH WITHIN HIM THAT MY LONG-DISTANCE PROBING...

...WILL NOT *INSTANTLY* MAKE HIM REVEAL THE LOCATION OF THE NEW REBEL BASE! STILL... HE IS *UNTRAINED!* THROUGH THIS CYBERNETIC LINK, HE SHALL *BEND* TO MY WILL...

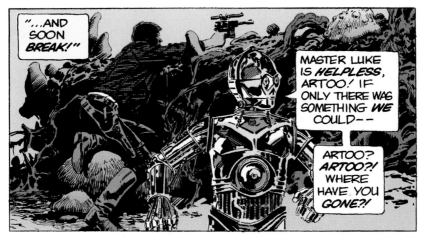

The golden droid and Han Solo soon see the **ANSWER!**

WAIT A MINUTE!

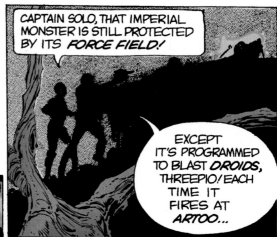

CAPTAIN SOLO, THAT IMPERIAL MONSTER IS STILL PROTECTED BY ITS *FORCE FIELD!*

EXCEPT IT'S PROGRAMMED TO BLAST *DROIDS*, THREEPIO! EACH TIME IT FIRES AT *ARTOO...*

...IT HAS TO *OPEN* THE SHIELD SLIGHTLY! TIMING...AIM...HAVE TO BE *PERFECT!* BUT...

Aboard the *EXECUTOR...*

YOUR SMALL, UNTRAINED DEFENSES ARE *CRUMBLING,* LUKE SKYWALKER! YOUR MIND IS ALMOST *OPEN* TO ME... *TOTALLY!*

YOU *DID* IT, CAPTAIN SOLO! SHOT THE IMPERIAL'S DRONE IN THE VERY *INSTANT* IT OPENED ITS FORCE FIELD TO BLAST ARTOO!

IT WAS OUR ONLY *CHANCE,* THREEPIO, BUT WHAT'S IT COST *LUKE?*

LUKE! ARE YOU?

I-I'M OKAY, HAN! BUT...DARTH VADER ALMOST *HAD* ME! EVEN REACHING ACROSS *SPACE*...

...HE'S SO MUCH *BETTER* WITH THE FORCE! I'M SO *UNTRAINED!*

BUT YOU'VE GOT MORE *FRIENDS* THAN HE'LL *EVER* HAVE, KID! WITH *THAT* GOIN' FOR YOU...

"...I'M BETTIN' YOU'LL *STILL* COME OUT AHEAD!'"

ALL SIGNALS ARE *DEAD*, LORD VADER!

LOST HIM *AGAIN!* CONTINUE LAUNCHING *PROBES!* PERHAPS ONE OF *THOSE* WILL DO WHAT WE FAILED TO ACCOMPLISH WITH OUR *TRAP* ON VERDANTH!

ARTOO-DETOO, YOUR ADVENTURING *SUCCEEDED*, BUT SOMEDAY IT'S GOING TO GET YOU IN *SERIOUS TROUBLE!*

C'MON, KID! LET'S GET BACK TO CHEWIE AND THE *FALCON*...WE'VE BEEN AWAY FROM HOTH AN' THE PRINCESS *LONG* ENOUGH!

The end... for now!

Cover #15 art by Al Williamson.

Cover #16 art by ~~~~~~~~.

Cover #17 art by Mark Schultz.

Cover #18 art by Kilian.

Cover #19 art by George Evans.

Cover #20 art by Al Williamson.